Victorians and the Machine

Victorians and the Machine

The Literary Response to Technology

Herbert L. Sussman

Harvard University Press Cambridge, Massachusetts 1968

To Elisabeth

Preface

In the last thirty years, the growing scholarly interest in the subject of technological change has given rise both to detailed histories of invention and to perceptive studies of the cultural effects of mechanization. In *Technics and Civilization,* Lewis Mumford presents a brilliant historical survey of the interrelationship between mechanical development and cultural change. In *Mechanization Takes Command,* Sigfried Giedion demonstrates the subtle ways in which the demands of the machine have altered the organic impulses of our nature. But the works of Mumford and Giedion proceed on a broad front. Although there has recently been published a study of the response of American culture to the machine, Leo Marx's *The Machine in the Garden,* there have been no detailed studies of the specific ways in which the English Victorians, the first people to live in a culture dominated by technology, expressed their realization that the use of the machine to perform certain physical tasks created profound changes in intellectual and emotional life.

In completing this work, I have received the generous assistance of many people. I would like to express my deepest thanks to Professor Howard Mumford Jones and Professor Jerome H. Buckley for their encouragement, interest, and astute criticism. I would also like to thank Professor Ulrich Knoepflmacher for his helpful comments on the manuscript. For assistance in the study of William Morris, I am indebted to Barbara Morris of the Victoria and Albert Museum, and to the Fitzwilliam Museum of Cambridge, England, the Victoria and Albert Museum, and Mr. John Brandon-Jones for permission to consult unpublished documents. I also wish to thank the President and Regents of the University of California for a fellowship providing the necessary time to complete this book.

The following quotations from Kipling are reprinted by permission of Mrs. George Bambridge, Doubleday & Company, Inc., Macmillan Co. of Canada Ltd., and Methuen & Co. Ltd.: lines from "A Song of the English," copyright 1909 by Rudyard Kipling; from "The Secret of the Machines," copyright 1911 by Rudyard Kipling; from "Tin Fish," copyright 1915 by Rudyard Kipling; from "Hymn of the Triumphant Airman," copyright 1927 by Rudyard Kipling; from "Song of the Dynamo," copyright 1928 by Rudyard Kipling; and from "Hymn of the Breaking Strain," copyright 1935 by Rudyard Kipling, all from *Rudyard Kipling's Verse: Definitive Edition*.

Berkeley, California   H.L.S.
June 1967

Contents

Victorians and the Machine

Were we required to characterise this age of ours by any single epithet, we should be tempted to call it, not an Heroical, Devotional, Philosophical, or Moral Age, but, above all others, the Mechanical Age. It is the Age of Machinery, in every outward and inward sense of that word.

—Thomas Carlyle,
"Signs of the Times"

Introduction

When the eight locomotives, drawing six hundred persons, including the Duke of Wellington, Robert Peel, and the ill-fated Mr. Huskisson, puffed down the tracks at the public opening of the Liverpool and Manchester Railway in 1830, high fences were erected, constables and soldiers called out "to keep off the pressure of the multitude, and prevent them from falling over in their eagerness to witness the opening ceremony."[1] Earlier technology had aroused no such general enthusiasm; for all their usefulness, the canal, the macadam road, the stagecoach were only refined versions of techniques that had existed from primitive times. But the steam locomotive, constructed almost wholly of iron, moving steadily along an iron track, throwing clouds of smoke and sparks into the air, was a sight entirely new to human experience. So, too, was the stationary engine, the steam engine without wheels, whose massive beam regularly rising and falling had become a familiar sight outside the red brick mills of northern cities. The technological revolution, then, differed from other historical events. Gods may change, churches remain very much the same; but the machine transformed the very appearance of the visible world. Not only was there the new machinery itself, there were now entire landscapes created by the machine: slag heaps, red brick factories, red brick houses for the factory workers. Even the countryside was marked by railway tracks, viaducts, and embankments.

The first question for the Victorian writer facing this new world was whether or not these images could be considered appropriate subjects for literature. And most often, the answer was no. With very few exceptions, during the Victorian period the machine appears in the minor works of major poets or the major works of minor poets.[2] Such poems as Charles Tennyson Turner's "Steam Threshing-Machine" or the "grooves of change" passage in his brother's "Locksley Hall" are distinct anomalies in Victorian poetry. The more typical attitude is that of William Morris who, for all his zeal in recasting the conditions of mechanized work, considered poetry a means of calling up a beauty vanished from the mechanized world:

> Forget six counties overhung with smoke,
> Forget the snorting steam and piston stroke,
> Forget the spreading of the hideous town;
> Think rather of the pack-horse on the down,
> And dream of London, small, and white, and clean.[3]

It was not until the very end of the nineteenth century

that Rudyard Kipling could advocate a new poetry celebrating the essential beauty of the machine.

Even the novelists, whom the Victorians felt should be more concerned with life as it is than as it might be, shied away from confronting the mechanized world. George Eliot writes *Middlemarch* as an historical novel set at the moment when the railway is about to disrupt the traditional order. The concern of Thackeray and Meredith is with the novel of society rather than the novel of industrial society. And Hardy follows the Wordsworthian theme of Victorian literature in finding the "essential passions of the heart" in people removed from the mechanized world. Thus, in the earlier part of the Victorian period the machine is found only in the novel of reform, in Dickens and the "industrial novelists." Only later in the century does there emerge, in H. G. Wells and in Kipling, prose fiction that celebrates technology and scientific speculation.

Primarily, the machine appears in those Victorian writers most directly concerned with immediate social problems. For Carlyle, Ruskin, and Morris, as well as for Dickens, Wells, and Kipling, the machine is important not merely as an image, a representation of a visual experience, but as a symbol, an image that suggests a complex of meanings beyond itself. For it is the fortuitous quality of the machine as symbol that it includes the central themes of Victorian culture. First, it was clear to all, from the compilers of Parliamentary blue-books to the worker watching the power loom, that technological progress was creating the immense social and economic upheavals taking place. As a metonymy for the constellation of changes that we, like the Victorians, call "progress," the machine, especially the railroad, was the most public, the most visual of emblems. As Mill says in his review of de Tocqueville's *Democracy in America*: "The mere visible fruits of scientific progress in a wealthy society, the mechanical improvements, the steam-engines, the railroads, carry the feeling of admiration for modern and disrespect for ancient times, down even to the wholly uneducated classes."[4]

Combined with the use of the machine as metonymy for progress was another perception, commonplace now only because it was first articulated by Victorian writers, that the rhythms created by the machine itself had a profound and primarily destructive effect on the psychic life. This idea, that as mechanization expands the affective life declines, shapes the form as well as the content of much Victorian writing. In its simplest form, it is the sense that the age is dull, and with ease has come softness; in a more subtle form, that the very qualities which make for the success of the machine, its power, its precision, its unwearied ability to repeat the same action, pose the greatest danger to the psyche. Literature consistently suggests that the rhythms of the machine are unnatural and, as such, destructive. The machine thus becomes both cause and symbol for what writers saw as the declining emotional vitality of their age.

But to use the machine as a symbol for what is unnatural is to evoke a complex of philosophical assumptions for which the machine is also symbol. Long before the railway and the power loom, in its primeval form as watch, to use Samuel Butler's evolutionary terms, the machine had served as a philosophical model. Modern scholarship defines romanticism as the replacing of this mechanistic intellectual model by another intellectual metaphor, that of the living organism.[5] The machine as metaphor for the cosmos implies a natural order, once created by a God, but now fixed, moving by regular laws and therefore deterministic; changing the metaphor to an organism suggests a developing universe, infused with a vital, usually divine, energy and therefore not subject to determinism. Applying the machine metaphor to the mind suggests that mental processes are orderly and therefore determined, and that the highest faculty is the reason; the organic metaphor suggests irregularity and freedom, a mind whose highest power is intuitive. The state as machine is also orderly, explicable by rationalistic laws; an organic society is free of restrictive external form, held together by ties of loyalty or love, and beyond rational creation or explanation.

In the sense that it consistently opposes the organic to the mechanistic, Victorian literature can be said to continue the romantic tradition. But if a major theme of Victorian writing is, like the earlier romantic literature, opposition to the deterministic, abstracting method of science, then the Victorians found this mechanistic mode of thought not only in abstract philosophical theory but manifested in the machine technology beginning to regulate their daily lives. In the Victorian period, the machine becomes simultaneously a tangible influence and a philosophical symbol.

And the opposition of the machine, considered in this double sense, to the organic becomes one of the dominant patterns in Victorian literature. A well-known passage from Mill's *On Liberty* gives explicit and eloquent expression to this theme:

> Supposing it were possible to get houses built, corn grown, battles fought, causes tried, and even churches erected and prayers said, by machinery—by automatons in human form—it would be a considerable loss to exchange for these automatons even the men and women who at present inhabit the more civilized parts of the world, and who assuredly are but starved specimens of what nature can and will produce. Human nature is not a machine to be built after a model, and set to do exactly the work prescribed for it, but a tree, which requires to grow and develop itself on all sides, according to the tendency of the inward forces which make it a living thing.[6]

The complexity in the use of the machine as symbol indicates a corresponding complexity in perception, an awareness that technological progress, the transformation of emotional life, and the growth of scientific thought are interdependent. For this new quality of life there is no single word. "Mechanization" applies to the tangible fact of technological progress, "mechanistic" to a mode of thought. Only the literary symbol of the machine can express this complex interrelationship which defines Victorian life; for, as symbol, it eradicates the misleading antithesis of external technological change to internal emotional and intellectual change. As Thomas Carlyle stated in 1829: "It is the Age of Machinery, in every outward and inward sense of that word."[7]

For many Victorian authors, this interrelation between the "outward and inward sense" becomes the central theme of their work. But it would be a mistake to see the literary response to the machine solely in terms of opposition. The proper metaphor for culture, as Lionel Trilling suggests,[8] is that of tension, the attempt to hold together contradictory ideas. And in confronting machine technology, the Victorians did hold directly contradictory ideas. The machine is both the unwearied iron servant and the sacrificial god to whom mankind has offered its soul. And as each writer criticizes the destructive union of mechanization and philosophic mechanism, he also admires his age for its technological skill. None are Luddites. Rather they see the machine as a servant who would be terribly useful if he would only not insist on ordering the household according to his own needs.

From this ambivalent attitude toward the machine develop the two antithetical literary modes of treating technology. Through nineteenth-century literature, as through nineteenth-century architecture,[9] there run two distinct styles, each of which can be defined by its attitude toward the machine. The first either attempts to escape what it considers the ugliness of the mechanized world or works in a realistic mode which describes this ugliness. The second, which culminates in Wells and Kipling, seeks to celebrate the machine in a language and through a set of values derived from the machine itself.

Examining the relationship between mechanistic thought and mechanization, whether in cosmology, aesthetic theory, the production of art, or biological science, is a central concern of Victorian intellectual prose. The conflict between the organic and the mechanistic, the new dangers and the new heroism of the machine age are major themes of Victorian imaginative writing. This study will discuss the literary forms developed to express these various, often ambivalent attitudes toward the machine and suggest that whatever consistency may be found in the Victorian literary response lies not so much in a dislike of technology as in a more general opposition to mechanistic modes of thought.

Although the symbolic implications of the machine remain generally consistent throughout the century, the imaginative treatment of the machine continued to change in response to advances in technology itself. Among the earliest visible signs of mechanization in England were the textile mills. But the Victorian vision of the mill surrounded by smoke and flame was not a reality until the stationary engine was first geared to provide the rotary motion necessary to turn spinning machinery. Early in the century, most mills depended upon water power and were thus confined to rural areas. The romantic poets, when they wrote of the machine at all, took up the contrast between the factory and its pastoral surroundings as a figure for what they saw as the profound unnaturalness of mechanization. In Blake the "dark, Satanic Mills" are seen destroying the divine, almost sacramental order of "England's green and pleasant Land."[10] In Wordsworth's *Excursion,* the textile mills of Cumberland destroy the natural rhythms once preserved in pastoral life:

> In full many a region, once like this
> The assured domain of calm simplicity
> And pensive quiet, an unnatural light
> Prepared for never-resting Labour's eyes
> Breaks from a many-windowed fabric huge.[11]

And the central theme of nineteenth-century machine literature, the destruction of the emotional life by mechanization, is expressed in the isolation of the child from the natural world. Wordsworth speaks of the child

> In whom a premature necessity
> Blocks out the forms of nature, preconsumes
> The reason, famishes the heart, shuts up
> The infant Being in itself, and makes
> Its very spring a season of decay![12]

But machine technology did not truly engage the literary imagination until the coming of the railway. Before the spread of the railway through England in the 1830's, steam-powered manufacturing was confined largely to the North, a long and difficult journey from London. The only signs of the machine in London itself before the railway arrived were a few steamboats on the Thames. But even after the railway connected North and South, few of the London-based writers had a felt sense of life in a mechanized factory or in the manufacturing towns. The standard picture of the industrial world in Victorian literature consists of smoke and flame seen from a distance. And of the machines themselves only the most fantastic or grotesque creations, such as the steam hammer or the stationary engine, caught the literary imagination.

But everyone understood the railway. It was, as Mill notes, the most public of symbols. The railway spread with amazing rapidity; the first company to use modern high-speed locomotives began operations in 1830, and by 1850 there were six thousand miles of track. But figures alone only suggest the extent of the railway revolution. Social life was transformed as travel became easy and inexpensive, economics transformed as the railway moved coal to the factories and finished products from the factory to the consumer. Add to this the new feeling of speed, the new optical sensations of railway travel and it becomes clear why most early Victorians saw theirs as the railway age.

But for all their novelty, for all their power, the stationary engine and the locomotive were unquestionably ugly. The stationary engine threw out clouds of smoke that hung over the industrial towns; railway passengers had to choose between suffocation and opening the windows to let in the soot and cinders. But the visual despair of the age of steam, which Lewis Mumford calls the Paleotechnic age,[13] began to lessen when, in the 1880's, the source of power shifted first from coal and steam to electricity and, finally, to the internal-combustion engine. So, for the late Victorians, Wells and Kipling, the image of the machine became the dynamo and the airplane. The new sleekness, above all the new cleanliness of the machine in, to use Mumford's term again,[14] the Neotechnic age did much to suggest to these later writers the possibilities of a literature celebrating the beauty of the machine.

In spite of the changing appearance of the machine, the attitudes toward it, from Carlyle to Wells, from Dickens to Kipling, remain generally consistent. This study, then, will concentrate on the work of seven writers who use the symbol of the machine to express the interrelationships of technological change, psychic well-being, and mechanistic thought. This emphasis on the effects of technological change necessarily omits major figures who express the more general Victorian literary opposition to mechanistic thought. The figure of the machine is central to Matthew Arnold's thought and rhetoric. When he asks in *Culture and Anarchy* "What is freedom but machinery? what is population but machinery? what is coal but machinery? what are railroads but machinery? what is wealth but machinery? what are, even, religious organisations but machinery?"[15] the figure points to the interdependence of the zeal for individualism, the decline of intellectual certainty, and the new wealth created by mechanized industry. And to "machinery" he opposes the organic process of culture, in which the mind grows by fusing ethics and intellect. But "machinery" remains primarily a metaphor. Arnold has little concern with the relation of technological change to the liberal ideology and even less with the psychological effects of mechanized labor. For him the villain is the Zeitgeist rather than the steam engine.

For similar reasons, Mill must be omitted also. For although the antithesis between the organic and the mechanistic pervades his writing, Mill, like Arnold, saw causal principles in political rather than technological terms. In *On Liberty,* individualism may be limned by its contrast to the figure of man as machine, but it is analyzed in its relation to majority rule, not to the factory system. But for Carlyle, Dickens, Ruskin, Morris, Butler, Wells, and Kipling, the belief that the tangible fact of mechanization shapes the intellectual, aesthetic, and emotional life of their time lies at the center of their thought and of their art.

Transcendentalism and the Machine: *Thomas Carlyle*

1

Thomas Carlyle and the railway both launched themselves upon England in the same decade. Both had spent their early years in obscurity in the North, the railway in primitive coal mines, Carlyle on a primitive Scottish farm. Both had aroused moderate public interest in the 1820's, but not until the 1830's had they each become famous. In 1830 the Liverpool and Manchester Railway opened, and in 1837 *The French Revolution* was published. But if the first locomotive prophesied the coming of a new era, Carlyle brought to England the ethics and the metaphysics of an old. At Edinburgh University he had been exposed to the doctrine of Newtonian science, to the idea that rather than divining the will of God, we need only consult the predictions of mathematicians—or perhaps of industrial engineers; for, as Carlyle realized, the scientific world view depends upon accepting the metaphor of the universe as a great machine, wholly material, orderly, predictable. From his very earliest writings, showing the capture of the intellect by its own self-created metaphors becomes a central method for Carlyle; in "Signs of the Times" he says: "This deep, paralysed subjection to physical objects comes not from Nature, but from our own unwise mode of *viewing* Nature."[1] And the central chapters of *Sartor Resartus* make very clear that the conversion from scientific materialism to transcendentalism depends upon exchanging one set of metaphors for another. Teufelsdröckh sounds the "Everlasting No" to a philosophy no longer limned with a mere watch but with the most modern technology: "To me the Universe was all void of Life, of Purpose, of Volition, even of Hostility: it was one huge, dead, immeasurable Steam-engine, rolling on, in its dead indifference, to grind me limb from limb. O, the vast, gloomy, solitary Golgotha, and Mill of Death! !"[2] To replace the analogy of the machine, Carlyle suggests another set of metaphors, organic and sacramental: "It is from this hour that I incline to date my Spiritual New-birth, or Baphometic Fire-baptism; perhaps I directly thereupon began to be a Man."[3]

And yet, although Carlyle rejected the machine as a philosophic metaphor, he was strongly attracted to the tangible iron and steel machines of his day. His exultation at the heroic labor of mechanized England is clear in the awed tones of an early letter describing Birmingham:

> Torrents of thick smoke, with ever and anon a burst of dingy flame, are issuing from a thousand funnels . . . You hear the clank of innumerable Steam-engines, the rumbling of cars and vans, and the hum of men inter-

rupted by the sharper rattle of some canal boat loading or disloading . . . I have looked into their iron works where 150,000 men are smelting the metal in a district a few miles to the north; their tubs and vats, as large as country churches, full of copperas and aqua fortis and oil of vitriol; and the whole is not without its attractions, as well as repulsions, of which when we meet, I will preach to you at large.[4]

But if the "attractions" of mechanization were intense, its "repulsions" were equally so. For to Carlyle, England's mechanization appeared bound to philosophical mechanism, the occupation with material means rather than spiritual ends. Drawn by his admiration of mechanized power, Carlyle sought to break this union by absorbing the machine into his transcendental philosophy, as philosopher showing the machine to be an emblem of transcendental power, and as social critic suggesting how technological progress could become a means of achieving transcendental ends. And even if Victorian industry eventually came to show little evidence of being in any way infused by divine energy, this symbolic mode of viewing the machine enabled Carlyle to become a seminal critic of his age.

i

Carlyle's study of German authors, especially Goethe, had so clarified his notion of history as a succession of distinct periods each shaped by a single idea[5] that when, in 1829, he turned to describe his own era, he naturally sought the single principle shaping the seemingly diverse phenomena. In "Signs of the Times," he first rejects the ideas that informed past eras; the nineteenth century is not an "Heroical, Devotional, Philosophical, or Moral Age."[6] Instead, he finds the unique historical principle in a material object considered symbolically: "It is the Age of Machinery, in every outward and inward sense of that word."[7] In using the term "machinery" in a double sense, in combining the "outward" meaning of technological progress with its "inward" meaning of mechanistic thought, Carlyle, writing in the year before the opening of the first railway, is not only presciently describing the temper of Victorian life but also setting up in "machinery" a complex symbol that Victorian writers will use to define their time. The symbolic mills of Coketown, mechanized work as representing modern slavery in the "Nature of Gothic," and Arnold's definition of Philistinism as love of "machinery" find a common origin in "Signs of the Times."[8]

In this work, Carlyle brings a persuasive concreteness to his discussion of historical forces and transcendental ideas by constant reference to specific early nineteenth-century technology. Although he had spent most of his early life on the farm or at the university, he was by no means unacquainted with the mechanization of pre-railway England. In Carlyle's day, Edinburgh University was the scientific center of the British Isles, and there he had taken the science course, showing some ability in mathematics. As a young man, he had journeyed with his friend Edward Irving to the New Lanark mills of Robert Owen, as well as to other English industrial cities. The Scottish lowlands, especially around

Glasgow, which he knew at first hand were, with Lancashire, the leading textile center of the British Isles. And
from the textile mills he took the specific machine
figures of the essay. For example, the figure of the "Machine of Society . . . as the grand working wheel from
which all private machines must derive, or to which
they must adapt, their movements,"[9] refers to the typical early textile mill in which each separate machine
was connected by a belt to a single rotating shaft turned
by either a water wheel or a stationary engine. The
"valves, and balances," by which the utilitarians hope
to rule over man's soul "as over a patent engine,"[10] suggest the parts of Watt's governor used to regulate the
speed of the steam engine. These particular mechanical
details could be used to symbolize the spirit of the age
because they were familiar to his audience. Even if the
readers of the *Edinburgh Review* had never been inside
a textile mill, they had almost surely seen pictures of
the stationary engine and spinning machinery; for the
demand for knowledge of the new technology was so
great in the early decades of the century as to call into
being the new profession of machine illustrator.[11]

This rhetorical fusion of the inward and outward
sense of machinery is exemplified in his first instance of
the mechanization of the spirit, education. After bringing contemporary educational reforms within the controlling metaphor, "we have machines for Education:
Lancastrian machines; Hamiltonian machines," he
elaborates the intellectual implications of the machine
figure: "Instruction, that mysterious communing of
Wisdom with Ignorance, is no longer an indefinable

tentative process, requiring a study of individual aptitudes, and a perpetual variation of means and methods,
to attain the same end; but a secure, universal, straightforward business, to be conducted in the gross, by proper
mechanism, with such intellect as comes to hand."[12] By
comparing Hamiltonian and Lancastrian methods of increasing the numbers of students taught to the methods
of the mechanized factory in the phrase "a secure, universal, straightforward business, to be conducted in the
gross," he is simultaneously showing that the educational reformers are emulating mechanized industry in
seeking to multiply output by standardizing product
and procedures, and pointing to the disparity between
these rationalized methods and the organic process
they are meant to regulate. A few sentences earlier he
notes that "nothing follows its spontaneous course,
nothing is left to be accomplished by old natural
methods."[13] Here, true education is defined as cultivating those "natural" qualities, "individual aptitudes,"
"perpetual variation," that distinguish organic from
inert matter, the child from cotton fiber. Furthermore,
here, as throughout his writing, he rejects the determinism implicit in the use of the machine metaphor;
education is "mysterious," "indefinable," not reducible
to quantitative terms.

Carlyle saw, too, that the immense productivity of
the new industry was accomplished not only by a more
efficient steam engine but also by the concentration of
capital, labor, and machinery into large, efficient units.
Throughout the essay, the metaphor of the machine suggests not so much the power of the new technology as

the rationalized organization it necessitates: "Philosophy, Science, Art, Literature, all depend on machinery . . . In defect of Raphaels, and Angelos, and Mozarts, we have Royal Academies of Painting, Sculpture, Music; whereby the languishing spirit of Art may be strengthened."[14] The creation of art is for Carlyle a "natural" process, dependent upon the sudden moment of intuition, the momentary vision of the divine: "Were Painting and Sculpture created by forethought, brought into the world by institutions for that end? No; Science and Art have, from first to last, been the free gift of Nature; an unsolicited, unexpected gift; often even a fatal one."[15] Applying the embodied logic of mechanized industry to the spontaneous operation of the imagination is not only irrelevant, but, as he judged from the feeble creative efforts of his day, destructive.

As a symbol of rationalized organization, the machine comes to suggest the general social changes occurring outside the factory. "Has any man, or any society of men, a truth to speak, a piece of spiritual work to do; they can nowise proceed at once and with the mere natural organs, but must first call a public meeting, appoint committees, issue prospectuses, eat a public dinner; in a word, construct or borrow machinery, wherewith to speak it and do it."[16] With the usual concrete references to the techniques of industrialism— here the creation of public support for a stock issue needed to purchase expensive machinery—and with the typical contrast between the organic and the mechanized, "natural organs" opposed to "machinery," Carlyle can create a metaphorical statement suggesting the combined effect of mechanistic thought and technological change in bringing about that phenomenon, so troubling to so many Victorians, the decline of individualism. In a new society forced into larger and larger units for the most efficient operation of the machine, the individual using his "natural organs" is, in Carlyle's phrase, as powerless as a "colony of Hindoo weavers squatting in the heart of Lancashire."[17]

But as social critic, Carlyle's interest does not stop with the "outward" social and economic effects of mechanization; his main concern is always the "inward sense" of mechanization, its effects on the psychic life. He sees the individual faced with the power of rationalized organizations ceasing to care, realizing that he cannot "accomplish the poorest enterprise single-handed and without mechanical aids," and thus losing his self-reliance in order to "make interest with some existing corporation."[18] The submergence of the individual in the organization, this dependence on "machinery" rather than the self becomes a major theme in Carlyle's critique of democracy.

As the essay moves into the political "signs of the times," the machine metaphor continues to suggest the combined power of mechanistic thought and mechanization in shaping Victorian life. It is primarily the metaphor itself, the patterning of political institutions on the efficient mechanized factory that Carlyle attacks. As one who saw transcendental ideas shaping the movements of history, Carlyle was sensitive to the power of metaphors in shaping institutions. Speaking of the central metaphor of the "Machine of Society," he states:

"Considered merely as a metaphor, all this is well enough; but here, as in so many other cases, the 'foam hardens itself into a shell,' and the shadow we have wantonly evoked stands terrible before us and will not depart at our bidding."[19] And yet Carlyle sees a partial truth in the machine analogy. Just as the Kantian sees the rational laws of science as useful in explaining the phenomenal world, so Carlyle sees mechanistic political thought as useful in the practical matters of government: "Civil government does by its nature include much that is mechanical, and must be treated accordingly."[20] What Carlyle is objecting to in the discussion of politics, as throughout the essay, is the application of rationalistic patterns to the organic processes of psychic life. And to suggest the tangible dangers of coldly logical Benthamism, Carlyle uses what was to become for the Victorians the chief figure for destructive rationality, the mechanized factory. The political economist, according to Carlyle, sees society as "the grand working wheel from which all private machines must derive, or to which they must adapt, their movements."[21] The crucial word for Carlyle here is "adapt," subordinate the spontaneity of impulse to the rationalized regularity of the mechanized system. Within the analogy of society as a machine, men must "adapt" their natural actions to the smooth order of the state, just as the worker must adapt his motion to the regular beat of the spinning machinery.

Continuing his attack on the Benthamites, Carlyle uses the figure of the worker as a machine, a comparison that will be made again and again throughout the century, to criticize the Benthamite assumption that men are as regular and as rational as the machines they tend. The Benthamites could never, Carlyle insists, "hope to comprehend the infinitudes of man's soul under formulas of Profit and Loss; and rule over this too, as over a patent engine, by checks, and valves, and balances."[22] The statement assumes the folly of applying the laws of science to the "infinitudes of man's soul," and assumes, too, the absurdity of the psychological determinism that follows from such rationalist assumptions. Only later in the century does biological science bring new proof against the vitalistic assumption that living things are not subject to the same natural laws as other phenomena. If the debate between a mechanistic and a vitalistic psychology is to be fought on "scientific" grounds in the latter part of the century, Carlyle in 1829 can refute psychological mechanism by an appeal to German transcendentalism. Just as he will attempt to justify his admiration of technology by seeing the machine as a creation of the spirit, so he can see philosophical mechanism, the categories of space, time, and causality, as creations of the higher reason: "For man is not the creature and product of Mechanism; but, in a far truer sense, its creator and producer."[23]

For Carlyle, then, the central intellectual danger of his day was not so much the practical success of mechanistic thought as the assumption that the machine metaphor could explain all phenomena. Like most Victorian writers, he distrusted the intellectual dependence upon scientific explanation: "the Metaphysical and Moral Sciences are falling into decay, while the Physical are engrossing, every day, more respect and attention."[24] For Carlyle the most important "metaphysical" questions were just those that lay beyond intellectual mechanism, that could not be answered by applying laws of material cause and effect. These he outlined with the usual metaphors of organic life and religious mystery as "the grand secrets of Necessity and Freewill, of the Mind's vital or non-vital dependence on Matter, of our mysterious relations to Time and Space, to God, to the Universe."[25]

And yet, as much as Carlyle may use the machine as symbol to relate the disturbing "signs of the times"— increasing organization, rationalized politics, philosophical determinism—the essay is hardly a tract for machine-breakers. Indeed, Carlyle is not being ironic here in his almost Macaulay-like praise of technological progress: "What wonderful accessions have thus been made, and are still making, to the physical power of mankind; how much better fed, clothed, lodged and, in all outward respects, accommodated men now are, or might be, by a given quantity of labour, is a grateful reflection which forces itself on every one."[26] But the machine images used to celebrate technology itself differ sharply from those used to attack intellectual mechanism. For when praised by Carlyle, the machine is no longer inert matter but takes on the qualities of life; it becomes spiritualized. "The shuttle drops from the fingers of the weaver, and falls into iron fingers that ply it faster. The sailor furls his sail, and lays down his oar; and bids a strong, unwearied servant, on vaporous wings, bear him through the waters."[27] The use of these vitalistic machine images in this early essay introduces the problem that runs throughout his work—how to celebrate technological progress while remaining true to transcendentalism or, to pose the question negatively, how to welcome the machine without accepting the methodology of science and the politics of Bentham. For aware as he is of the error in applying the analogy of the machine to the operation of the spirit, he is quite eager to retain the benefits of the machine in the physical world. In "Signs of the Times," rather than renouncing machine technology entirely, he appeals for balance between what he calls "Mechanism" and the "Dynamical," between technological skill and an ultimately transcendental moral sense:

> Undue cultivation of the inward or Dynamical province leads to idle, visionary, impracticable courses, and, especially in rude eras, to Superstition and Fanaticism, with their long train of baleful and well-known evils. Undue cultivation of the outward, again, though less immediately prejudicial, and even for the time productive of many palpable benefits, must, in the long-run, by destroying Moral Force, which is the parent of all other Force, prove not less certainly, and perhaps still more hopelessly, pernicious. This, we take it, is the grand characteristic of our age.[28]

ii

It is impossible for the modern mind, so accustomed to accelerating technological change, to recapture the wonder that the new technology created in the eighteen twenties, thirties, and forties. This awe Carlyle could not help but share. To get from Ecclefechan to the university he had had to walk for days carrying his few possessions over his shoulder. On his first two trips to London, he had taken a slow ship to Liverpool and an even slower stagecoach to the capital. His first railway ride, taken in 1839 on the new line between London and Preston, was, then, an event wholly beyond his previous experience:

> To whirl through the confused darkness, on those steam wings, was one of the strangest things I have experienced—hissing and dashing on, one knew not whither . . . We went over the tops of houses—one town or village I saw clearly, with its chimney heads vainly stretching up towards us—*under* the stars; not under the clouds but among them. Out of one vehicle into another, snorting, roaring we flew: the likest thing to a Faust's flight on the Devil's mantle; or as if some huge steam night-bird had flung you on its back, and was sweeping through unknown space with you, most probably toward London.[29]

Even in this personal letter, as in "Signs of the Times," the machine as the helper of man takes the attributes of organic life; the locomotive is not a manifestation of engineering skill, but a great bird bearing the passengers along with vitalistic energy.

This straightforward delight in technological power became morally justified for Carlyle by the principle that he shared with his age and, indeed, articulated for it, the doctrine of work. In his youth he had learned from his Calvinist parents that the ceaseless round of farm labor was not an unfortunate necessity, but a moral imperative. The distinction between the value of work and the danger of thought runs through his writing: "How one loves to see the burly figure of him, this thick-skinned, seemingly opaque, perhaps sulky, almost stupid Man of Practice, pitted against some light adroit Man of Theory."[30] This anti-intellectualism led him to admire the early nineteenth-century technologists, who, as Carlyle correctly saw, had worked without the benefit of theoretical science. Carlyle's heroes of industry are men like James Brindley, the canal-builder, and Richard Arkwright, the inventor of the spinning jenny, who, untutored in physical science, built canals and textile mills by combining an intuitive sense of how things ran with simple hard work. The doctrine of work was always the standard by which Carlyle judged the technological revolution, and although he feared the ability of organized industry to stifle the individual voice, he could only admire its gathering of multitudes to perform the duty of labor. He recounts with almost religious reverence "the awakening of a Manchester, on Monday morning, at half-past five by the clock; the rushing-off of its thousand mills, like the boom of an Atlantic tide, ten-thousand times ten-thousand spools and spindles all set humming there."[31]

In his response to the machine, Carlyle appears the perfect illustration of Max Weber's thesis that the doctrine of earthly vocation as a "calling" enabled the Calvinist to channel his spiritual energies into the activities of capitalism. For Carlyle, the machine appeared as a material tool for fulfilling God's purposes. And in his rhetoric it is consistently used within transcendental terms as a symbol, a physical manifestation of corresponding spiritual forces. The triumph of technology is but an emblem, if we read the spiritual sign correctly, not of self-seeking commercialism, but of the Godlike soul in man: "Ye have shivered mountains asunder, made the hard iron pliant to you as soft putty . . . on Firehorses and Windhorses ye career. Ye are most strong. Thor red-bearded, with his blue sun-eyes, with his cheery heart and strong thunder-hammer, he and you have prevailed."[32] Even cotton spinning becomes an episode in a spiritual crusade, "the triumph of man over matter."[33] As the emblem of transcendental purposes, the machine becomes a figure not for causal determinism, but for the power of the higher reason to control and order the seemingly deterministic world; the machine is the weapon by which man can do "personal battle with Necessity, and her dark brute Powers, to make them reasonable and serviceable."[34]

Seeing the machine as symbol of the spirit enabled Carlyle to welcome the machine while excluding intellectual mechanism. To accept technology while rejecting scientists, he brings the inventor into the context of Carlylean heroism. For Carlyle invention depends less on the practical understanding than on that perception of transcendental laws which is the essential quality of the hero. He describes James Watt working on the steam engine with imagery more appropriate to Faust calling up the earth-spirit than a practical Scotsman tinkering with the atmospheric engine; while the aristocrats were busy shooting partridges, "this man with blackened fingers, with grim brow, was searching out, in his workshop, the Fire-secret."[35] Watt's engine becomes a transcendental machine, not "huge, dead" like the steam engine symbolizing intellectual mechanism in the "Everlasting No," but the "Scottish Brassmith's IDEA . . . travelling on fire-wings round the Cape . . . on all hands unweariedly fetching and carrying."[36] The word "IDEA," capitalized for emphasis, has here the Coleridgean sense of transcendental energy realizing itself in the material world. Inventors are seen as holy men who can fathom mysterious spiritual forces. They are wizards, magicians: "Prospero can send his Fire-Demons panting across all oceans."[37] As interpreters of the transcendental, technologists take their place in the English pantheon: "England was not only to have had her Shakespeares, Bacons, Sydneys, but to have her Watts, Arkwrights, Brindleys! We will honour greatness in all kinds."[38]

The accomplishments of the hero as inventor, however symbolic of higher forces, were, unfortunately, only too visible to the naked eye. And yet Carlyle's notion of the transcendental machine allowed him to become one of the few Victorians to find any aesthetic pleasure in the industrial landscape. Most writers and painters confronted a visual world their theories could not encompass. When the machine first began to transform the English countryside in the latter eighteenth century, beauty was still conventionally associated with certain subjects, notably the pastoral landscape.[39] But what was to be done with the foundries and cotton mills that appeared in the middle distance? Most artists, as well as most romantic poets, merely ignored the factories and described those landscapes still undefiled, or, like

Wordsworth, wrote poetry protesting the act of desecration.[40] A few landscape painters, however, did include the new mills, but managed to absorb them into the pastoral scene. In "Arkwright's Cotton Mill at Cromford,"[41] painted in 1789 by Joseph Wright of Derby, the building seen at night is set far in the background, the glow of its windows dimmed by the moon, and the entire mill dominated by the trees and rustic cart of the foreground. The factory has not yet destroyed the pastoral order of England. In the days when water-wheels provided the chief source of power, mills were established in remote rural areas, and the painter and the poet could still portray the soothing effect of nature on mechanized work, rather than, as later writers would, the destruction of the pastoral world by the machine. In describing a rural mill in "Corn-Law Rhymes," Carlyle praises the effect of nature in meliorating the harsh conditions of mechanized work: "It is a rustic, rude existence; barren moors, with the smoke of Forges rising over the waste expanse. Alas, no Arcadia; but the actual dwelling-place of actual toil-grimed sons of Tubalcain; yet are there blossoms, and the wild natural fragrance of gorse and broom; yet has the Craftsman pauses in his toil."[42]

To all artists, the machine was new and, being new, fearful, as capable of arousing the shudder of fear as a storm or mountain crag. And so in the nineteenth century there developed from the older convention of the sublime a new form, the technological sublime. A typical example is "Iron Works at Coalbrook Dale," executed before 1800 by Philip James de Loutherbourg.[43] In this painting of an early iron foundry, flames rise through the narrow valley, their source hidden to increase the sense of mystery. The smoke swirls into and mingles with the overhanging clouds to suggest a fearful power in technology that matches the primeval power of the wooded cliffs.

This same convention of the technological sublime controls Carlyle's description of the mechanized landscape, a scene he did not find beautiful in itself but, to the mind attuned to its symbolic import, capable of arousing a fearful awe. To him, Manchester is not beautiful in its surface appearance, but "wonderful . . . fearful."[44] The energy it manifests is equated with the power of nature: Manchester "is perhaps, if thou knew it well, as sublime as a Niagara, or more so."[45] This emphasis on the response of the viewer to the scene's symbolism rather than its appearance enables Carlyle to find a particular form of beauty in mechanized England. Although the industrial scene may be ugly (he calls Manchester a "noisome wrappage") and must be tailored into the proper clothing for the emerging historical forces so as to "leave the beauty free and visible there,"[46] it still has, to Carlyle, a transcendental or symbolic beauty as the embodiment of the sacrament of productive labor.

This sense of the machine as symbol enables Carlyle to concentrate on the power of mechanized industry, but it excludes any attempt to find beauty in the forms of the machine itself. And yet, looking through the outward appearance of the machine to its symbolic import was the most natural aesthetic for the early industrial period; for the age of iron, steam, and soot was ugly by any standard and only by subordinating this tangible ugliness in order to convey the power and revolutionary quality of the machine could the artist succeed. One of the few enduring Victorian paintings of the machine, Turner's "Rain, Steam and Speed," also blurs the specific details of steam technology in order to emphasize its power. In this example of the technological sublime, the forms of the locomotive and the smoke merge into the storm, thus equating the steam with the violent forces of nature and emphasizing not the beauty of functional design but the power of the engine. Even in the twentieth century, the only aesthetic pleasure that can be derived from the last survivals of the Paleotechnic age—the steel mills of Gary, Indiana, for example, or a railway switching yard—lies in seeing in their ugliness a frightening symbol of industrial power, a modern type of the sublime.

Reinforcing Carlyle's spiritualizing of the machine is his assurance that technological progress is the unfolding of a transcendental historical necessity in the material world. In the familiar equation of Progress with Providence, he describes the causes of the industrial revolution, by which he means the inspired revelations of the inventors, as "inevitable every one of them; foreseen, not unexpected, by Supreme Power; prepared, appointed from afar. Advancing always through all centuries, in the middle of the eighteenth they *arrived*."[47] Even in the green and pleasant land of the twelfth century, a world Carlyle looked to with nostalgia, the spiritual seed of the machine age is but waiting to germinate. "Saint Mungo rules in Glasgow; James Watt still slumbering in the deep of Time . . . The Centuries are big; and the birth hour is coming, not yet come."[48]

Mixed with Carlyle's trust in Providence is a strong stiffening of simple patriotism. Within his transcendental rhetoric, England becomes a hero among nations, its technological skill a sure sign of its election to a divine mission, and its mechanization the culmination of its spiritual development:

> Who shall say what work and works this England has yet to do? For what purpose this land of Britain was created, set like a jewel in the encircling blue of Ocean; and this Tribe of Saxons fashioned in the depths of time . . . No man can say: it was for a work, and for works, incapable of announcement in words. Thou seest them there; part of them stand done, and visible to the eye; even these thou canst not *name:* how much less the others still matter of prophecy only![49]

But Carlyle's attempt to reconcile mechanization and transcendentalism is more a rhetorical than an intellectual success. In emphasizing the role of intuition in the development of technology, Carlyle illustrates the denigration of intellect that will distort the aesthetic response to the machine throughout the century. Furthermore, the description of the machine as transcendental symbol serves to persuade the reader not only of the inevitability but also the moral rightness of mechanization. In part the reason for Carlyle's immense influence is just this rhetorical ability to ennoble what men already believed. For stripped of their spiritual clothing, his attitudes toward mechanization differ little from the most common Victorian defenses of the machine. The prophecy of England as a hero among nations is but a transcendental figure for Victorian chauvinism. The trope of technology as a victory of the higher reason over the enslaving phenomenal world merely spiritualizes the Baconian praise of the technological conquest of nature. And the description of technological progress as the unfolding of transcendental historical forces restates the common equation of England's progress with God's will. But even if Carlyle was to realize in his later writings that the steam engine had become less an emblem of the spirit than a device for turning cotton into clothing at a high profit, this vision of the transcendental machine, of mechanical progress spiritualized, shapes his incisive social criticism.

iii

At the center of Carlyle's social thought is his faith that England's mechanization is the natural, inevitable unfolding of historical necessity. He saw history as periodic, an organic era gradually disintegrating to be replaced, after a transitional period, by another organic period held together by a new principle. This view of periodicity enabled him to perceive the idea of "machinery" shaping both the intellect and society; it also kept him, as social critic, from the common Victorian response, exemplified by his disciple Ruskin, of seeking to reverse history by moving back to a pastoral society. Always believing the present to be a transitional period preceding a fully industrialized future, he looked to a highly organized state as the best means of mitigating what he felt to be temporary social dislocations.

From his personal observation and his energetic study of Parliamentary bluebooks during the 1830's and 1840's, Carlyle had become increasingly aware of the "Condition of England," a condition he diagnosed as being caused by the machine. But of the innumerable effects of technological change, his writing concentrates on one, unemployment. As idleness is the unforgivable personal sin, so enforced idleness is the unforgivable social sin, for it subverts the main moral purpose of mechanization, the increased opportunity for work. The picture of men anxious to labor yet unable to find jobs is for Carlyle "the saddest sight that Fortune's inequality exhibits under this sun."[50] Just this sight, able-bodied men nodding in Fen-country poorhouses, had turned Carlyle from his research on Cromwell to writing social criticism.

His complex perception of technological unemployment is consistently expressed through an equally complex use of the machine metaphor. He says:

> It is consistent that the wages of "skilled labour," as it is called, should in many cases be higher than they ever were: the giant Steamengine in a giant English Nation will here create violent demand for labour, and will there annihilate demand. But, alas, the great portion of labour is not skilled: the millions are and must be skilless, where strength alone is wanted; ploughers, delvers, borers; hewers of wood and drawers of water; menials of the Steamengine, only the *chief* menials and immediate *body*-servants of which require skill.[51]

The personified steam engine here suggests that since a stationary engine, unlike a water wheel, could be established anywhere that railways could bring it coal, industry could move about the country in response to economic conditions, thus creating sudden changes in the need for labor within any specific locality. Furthermore, the figure shows that whereas the machine has decreased the need for workers whose only qualification is their strength, it has increased the need for skilled laborers to care for it. With these specific economic suggestions, the figure of the machine as a powerful ruler waited upon by human servants, a figure that appears frequently throughout the century, suggests the psychological effect of subordinating not only economic activity but also natural impulse to the demand of the machine.

For all his awareness of the tangible effects of mechanization, Carlyle never saw social dislocation as a purely economic problem. One of the great strengths of his social criticism is his ability to see the inward as well as the outward sense of "Machinery," to comprehend the emotional effects of technological change. Since work was always to him a psychological necessity as well as a moral duty, his descriptions of unemployment dwell not so much on physical as on mental suffering. Describing the effect of mechanization in making the factory worker dependent on the whims of buyers around the world, he emphasizes the psychological rather than the economic result: "English Commerce with its world-wide convulsive fluctuations, with its immeasurable Proteus Steam-demon, makes all paths uncertain for them, all life a bewilderment."[52] Or commenting on the general dislocations created by the machine, he again emphasizes emotional stability: "Sobriety, steadfastness, peaceable continuance, the first blessings of man, are not theirs."[53] Indeed, Carlyle's entire critique of industrial society is set in a psychological frame. Gurth the swineherd is "happy" with "the certainty of supper and social lodging," happy with "the inexpressible satisfaction of feeling himself related indissolubly, though in a rude brass-collar way, to his fellow-mortals in this Earth,"[54] happier in a stable authoritarian society where he is insulated from the insecurity and isolation faced by the industrial worker forced to compete for jobs in a rapidly changing society.

This explanation of social unrest in terms of a psychological malaise caused by the nature of mechanized work becomes a major theme in the literary response to the machine, notably in Dickens and in Morris. But for Carlyle the psychic remedy lay in work, any kind of work, even machine work. As a duty, as a moral obligation, work is to be performed with tight-lipped determination in order to please God, not in order to feel the sensuous pleasure of creativity. There is in Carlyle's writings none of the sense implicit in Ruskin and explicit in Morris that machine work must be made more satisfying for the worker. Even his attack on the quality of machine-made goods is moral rather than aesthetic. If the results of labor are the measure of devotion to the task, then shoddy products indicate a laxness in performing the ethical imperative of work.

In the diatribe on "cheap and nasty" in "Shooting Niagara," the voice is that of the outraged moralist: "You are not to purchase, to make or to vend any ware or product of the 'cheap and nasty' genus, and cannot in any case do it without sin, and even treason against the Maker of you,—consider what a *quantity* of sin, of treason, petty and high, must be accumulating in poor England every day!"[55] Carlyle is not pointing here to the distortion of psychic life under the repetitive rhythm of the machine, but to the commercial spirit that violates the ethic of work in the hope of quick profit.

To Carlyle, the entire process of mechanization seemed to have slipped away from any concern with ethical ends. The purpose of his social criticism is to prove that with the proper clothing the inevitable mechanization of England may body forth its true nature as a moral endeavor. To this end, Carlyle saw the first necessity as bringing order to the uncontrolled development of the machine. For the early Carlyle, the Carlyle of "Chartism" and *Past and Present,* this order is not an end in itself, but a means of developing the ethical values inherent in mechanization. The idealized medieval society he contrasts to industrial England is pre-eminently a well-ordered world, with all the emotional solace discipline can bring, but the order imposed by Abbot Samson enables the monks by working peaceably and fruitfully to serve God. And "Laborare est orare" is to be the motto of the factory system as well.[56] For Carlyle, industrial society becomes an immense monastic order, complete with discipline and self-sacrifice, capable of including the entire population. All

Carlyle's specific reforms become persuasive in their analogy to religious institutions. Even emigration, as advocated in "Chartism," becomes a new crusade in which an army of workers will set spirit against matter in some primitive part of the globe.

The main responsibility for revealing the ethical ends implicit in the technological means lay with the "captain of industry." Like the hero as inventor, the hero as industrialist is to be the transmitter of the divine to the material world, the prophet of the transcendental purpose emerging through mechanization. But in describing the industrial utopia achieved by the captain of industry, Carlyle is again careful to separate industrial mechanization and intellectual mechanism; his metaphor for society is not the machine, but organic life. He envisions "immense Industrial Ages, as yet all inorganic, and in a quite pulpy condition, requiring desperately to harden themselves into some organism."[57] The coming machine age is to be an organic era, informed by the principle of an ethical industrialism. For the ethos itself, Carlyle again uses organic figures. In *Sartor Resartus* he speaks of "organic filaments" and in *Past and Present* points to the inescapable ethical responsibility of society in a brilliant figure cast in specifically biological terms, the Irish widows who "have to prove their relationship by dying of typhus-fever."[58] For the rationalized and impersonal contract system, Carlyle hopes to substitute an emotional bond of loyalty between master and men that would be impervious to the material necessity of economics. In response to the beneficence of his employer, the worker's natural feeling of reverence for superior man would emerge and with this reverence would return the natural feelings of religious awe.

But Carlyle's vision of a mechanized utopia set to God's purposes by God's agents on earth was hardly fulfilled by the Victorian industrialists. And this no one realized more clearly than Carlyle. By the time of the publication of *Latter-Day Pamphlets* in 1850, the call to realize the transcendental purposes of mechanization had become lost in his criticism of the materialistic age of machinery as it existed in the present. The ethical failure of industrialism seemed to Carlyle to be illustrated in the inability of the age to produce industrial heroes. There are only anti-heroes such as George Hudson, the "railway king." In the essay "Hudson's Statue" he is the target of Carlyle's wrath because he typifies the hero *manqué* created by mechanization, the leader who is forceful, effective, admired, but lacking any awareness of the ethical potential of the machine. His emblem then does not combine the divine and the material, as does the "Laborare est orare" of the monks. But here Carlyle treats the symbol of the machine in a mock-heroic way, much as Ruskin does in "Traffic," to emphasize the divorce of mechanization and ethics. He suggests that the proposed statue show the railway king "mounted on some figure of a Locomotive, garnished with Scrip-rolls proper."[59]

As his final disillusionment indicates, Carlyle could praise the machine only as an instrument of a dimly perceived ethical purpose. And yet, paradoxically, Carlyle's own social reforms, for all their original moral force and transcendental sanction, appear, with the ever useful help of hindsight, to be as dangerous as any simple Victorian commercialism. As clearly as any Victorian, Carlyle saw the anomie that is the price of an atomistic technological society. He said: "Isolation is the sum-total of wretchedness to man. To be cut off, to be left solitary: to have a world alien, not your world; all a hostile camp for you; not a home at all, of hearts and faces who are yours, whose you are! It is the frightfullest enchantment."[60] To allay this sense of isolation, Carlyle sought in mechanized work a binding spiritual purpose for the nineteenth century similar to the integrating religious faith of the twelfth. If the ethical value of factory work is no longer self-evident, even on psychological grounds, the doctrine of work can do little to create a humane industrialized society, for it ignores the conditions of work itself; Carlyle is not, for example, at all concerned with child labor. Only with the radical attack on the ethic of work itself by Morris can the machine be seen as a means of achieving psychic richness.

To set men to the duty of work, Carlyle looked to an authoritarian state. In the 1830's and 1840's, the authority of the industrial leader is the means of restoring some benevolence to a system predicated solely on self-interest. But by the 1850's, seeing his ideal of an ethical industrialism confuted, Carlyle came to consider the power and discipline of the industrial army as an end in itself. As this final movement to authoritarianism indicates, unable to move beyond the traditional values of Calvinism and German transcendentalism, Carlyle could not find for the machine a purpose beyond the purely material.

2   The Industrial Novel and the Machine: *Charles Dickens*

To the early Victorian writer, the mechanized world presented a countenance of unquestioned ugliness. Even if he shared Carlyle's vision of an emergent spiritual beauty, he found little aesthetic inspiration in the smoke of the steam engine and the roar of the loom. Then, as now, mechanized industry was described less to celebrate its beauty than to urge its reform. But even in the industrial novel, the writer was forced to create, *a nihilo,* a literary language to describe the machine. Most often, the new is seen in terms of the old; the machine becomes the tenor of the metaphor rather than the vehicle. The factory is the Inferno, the engine an immense animal. Alone among the industrial novelists, indeed alone among English writers of prose fiction up to Wells and Kipling, Dickens' imagination had so absorbed machine technology that he could use it as vehicle rather than tenor,[1] as a complex symbol for the combination of industrial mechanization and mechanistic thought that he, like Carlyle, saw as the shaping principle of Victorian life.

i

Dickens began his literary career in the same decade that machine technology came to dominate English life. Like Carlyle, he had grown up among the sights and the customs of an England that was closer to the eighteenth century than to the mechanized nineteenth. His youth was spent in and around a London virtually unblemished by the new technology.[2] The railway did not reach there from Birmingham until 1838, two years after Dickens' sudden fame with *Pickwick*. Before the railway, the main signs of the technological revolution were a few steamboats on the Thames, for the lack of adequate transportation confined steam-powered industry to areas nearer the coal fields of the North. As a boy, Dickens himself had experienced the dull round of routinized work, but in a typically preindustrial establishment where small boys pasted labels on blacking bottles by hand. In his education at Rochester, then a quiet cathedral town, and on his assignments as stenographer in the ecclesiastical courts and the unreformed Parliament, he absorbed the atmosphere of the old England that was to be the typical background of his novels. His work as a reporter took him only on occasional and brief trips to the manufacturing towns of the North, still a long and uncomfortable journey by stagecoach. For Dickens then, as for his generation, the fact of ceaseless technological change, which future generations were to accept unquestioned, came to a mind already formed and mixed rather uneasily with notions derived from an earlier time. If Carlyle responded to the new technology with the Calvinist values of his youth, Dickens also looked to the past in commenting on the present. The myth of pastoral England, the organic society shattered by industrialism, remains the standard of value throughout his novels.

And yet, for Dickens, as for all the Victorian writers, this longing for a simpler and more humane past was constantly challenged by the excitement he felt in the new technology. Addressing a meeting in Birmingham in 1844, Dickens told of his railway journey there with an old man "who expressed himself most mournfully as to the ruinous effects and rapid spread of railways, and was most pathetic upon the virtues of the slow-going old stage-coaches." Dickens, "entertaining some little lingering kindness for the road," had politely agreed with his companion and joined him in bemoaning the bumps and jolts, the screeches and shocks of a Victorian train ride. He found, however, that "when the speed of the engine was abated, or there was the slightest prolongation of our stay in any station, the old gentleman was up in arms, and his watch was instantly out of his pocket, denouncing the slowness of our progress." Dickens then compared this old man to those who declaim "against the vices and crimes of society and at the same time are the first and foremost to assert that vice and crime have not their common origin in ignorance and discontent."[3] If the old man's relation to the opponents of education is tenuous, his similarity to the storyteller is strong, for he exemplifies Dickens' own ambivalent response to machine technology. Dickens, who perceived not only the physical suffering but also the psychological hazards brought by the machine, was, like the figure in his story, unable to restrain his fascinated interest in the speed of technological progress.

Although Dickens' pride in the industrial present was quite as strong as Carlyle's, his mind was not given to visionary social schemes. Rather than dreaming of industrial utopias, his eye fixed on details of the here and now, and he most often applauded the prosaic virtues of efficiency and convenience, as in this description of the new through-train service to Paris: "What has the South Eastern [Railway] done with all the horrible little villages we used to pass through in the *Diligence?* . . . Where are the two-and-twenty weary hours of long day and night journey, sure to be either insupportably hot or insupportably cold?" He marveled too at the minutiae of railway organization: "I paid 'through to Paris' at London Bridge, and discharged myself of all responsibility, except the preservation of a voucher ruled into three divisions, of which the first was snipped off at Folkestone, the second aboard the boat, and the third taken at my journey's end."[4] These details of cross-Channel travel were made glorious by their newness. To express his sense of wonder, Dickens could only compare the new to the old, the mechanized event to the ancient tale of magic. He concludes by "blessing the South Eastern Company for realising the Arabian Nights in these prose days."

Other industrial novelists, too, expressed their sense of the almost preternatural quality of the new technology by invoking the wonders of *The Arabian Nights*. Disraeli's Coningsby, awe-struck on his first visit to Manchester, "entered chambers vaster than are told of in Arabian fable, and peopled with habitants more wondrous than Afrite or Peri. For there he beheld, in long-continued ranks, those mysterious forms full of existence without life, that perform with facility, and in an instant, what man can fulfil only with difficulty and in days."[5] In Mrs. Gaskell's *North and South*, Mr. Hale, a product of Oxford and a country parsonage, now a tutor in humanities to an industrialist, on hearing of "the magnificent power, yet delicate adjustment of the might of the steam-hammer," recalls "some of the wonderful stories of subservient genii in the Arabian Nights—one moment stretching from earth to sky and filling all the width of the horizon, at the next obediently compressed into a vase small enough to be born in the hand of a child."[6] This use of the technological sublime to create a sense of awe at the power of the machine rather than an appreciation of its functional beauty persists throughout the century, finally culminating in Kipling's attempt at the end of the century to create a new literature based on the romance of the machine.

As the editor of successful periodicals, Dickens sought to bring the romance of technology to his readers. He wrote to his managing editor:

> I want a great paper done, on the distribution of Titles in England. It would be a very remarkable thing to take the list of the House of Peers, the list of Baron-

ets and Knights, and (without personality) divide the more recent titles into classes and ascertain what they were given *for*. How many chemists, how many men of Science, how many writers, how many aldermen.
How much intellect represented.
How much imagination.
How much learning.
How much expression of the great progress of the country. How much of Railway construction, of Electric Telegraph discovery, of improvements in machinery, of any sort of contribution to the happiness of mankind.[7]

This article was never written, but *Household Words* abounds with other articles on the wonders of the new technology, such as "Ballooning," "The Planet-Watchers of Greenwich," "The Stereoscope," "The Power Loom," "Electric Light,"[8] along with innumerable articles on the railway. Nor did Dickens' magazines hesitate to criticize technological progress with articles ranging from jibes at station refreshment stands to a serious campaign demanding the fencing off of industrial machinery. Yet even the criticism in *Household Words* implicitly accepts the machine age and points only to superficial details requiring adjustment.

The enthusiastic response to the machine in the periodicals is not due solely to Dickens' shrewd catering to his public's interest in things mechanical. Rather, the medium of popular journalism provided an outlet for his own deep pride in machine technology. The same delight in the practical and the material which pervades *Household Words* also characterizes his personal reaction to the sights of America and the European continent.

He thrilled to the grandeur of the Alps and the exertion of crossing mountain passes in the dead of winter, but the artistic glories of past civilizations left him unmoved. In his travels, as in his writing, he showed no longing for the aesthetic values destroyed by the mechanized world. With the complacency of his own Mr. Podsnap, he most appreciated the scenes that reminded him of England. To John Forster he wrote: "This [Turin] is a remarkably agreeable place. The contrast this part of Italy presents to the rest is amazing. Beautifully made railroads, admirably managed; cheerful, active people; spirit, energy, life, progress."[9]

His delight in modern invention gives imaginative vitality to his descriptions of familiar machine forms. Numerous passages refute Gissing's assertion that "never is Dickens more joyously himself than when he tells of stagecoach and posting vehicles. He tried his hand at a description of the railway, but with no such gusto, no such success."[10] Train rides, in fact, often inspired Dickens, and the railroad carriage, he wrote, was "always a wonderfully suggestive place to me when I am alone."[11] His joyful picture of the confusion at "Mugby Junction" is just one example of his "gusto" in depicting the railway:

> Then was heard a distant ringing of bells and blowing of whistles. Then, puppet-looking heads of men popped out of boxes in perspective, and popped in again. Then, prodigious wooden razors, set up on end, began shaving the atmosphere. Then, several locomotive engines in several directions began to scream and be agitated. Then, along one avenue a train came in. Then, along another two trains appeared that didn't come in, but

stopped without. Then, bits of trains broke off. Then,
a struggling horse became involved with them. Then,
the locomotives shared the bits of trains, and ran away
with the whole.[12]

The same vigor fills his rare magazine descriptions of
industrial machinery, as in this portrait of the devices
used to construct ironclad warships:

> The mechanical powers for piercing the iron plates—
> four inches and a half thick—for rivets, shaping them
> under hydraulic pressure to the finest tapering turns of
> the ship's lines, and paring them away, with knives
> shaped like the beaks of strong and cruel birds, to the
> nicest requirements of the design! . . . "Obedient
> monster, please to bite this mass of iron through and
> through, at equal distances, where these regular chalk-
> marks are, all round." Monster looks at its work, and
> lifting its ponderous head, replies, "I don't particularly
> want to do it; but if it must be done—!"[13]

Yet, for all their imaginative power, Dickens' accounts of technology in his occasional writing are merely
isolated descriptive pieces, filled with pride and wonder
because Dickens as journalist is only considering the
machine in itself, not as part of its social and moral
environment. But once these vivid evocations of technology are placed within a social context, as in *Dombey
and Son* and *Hard Times,* the machine becomes a symbol for the sins of society as a whole. This movement
toward the machine as the emblem of social evil is seen
most clearly in the treatment of the steamboat in his
first and last completed works.

He first mentions steam power in a piece from
Sketches by Boz entitled "The River." The subject is

the excursion steamers that carried entire families on holiday outings and returned working husbands to their families vacationing at Margate. The wharf, he says, is "one of the most amusing places we know."[14] On the ship, Dickens observes two men watching the engine and discussing the implications of steam: " 'Wonderful thing steam, Sir.' 'Ah! (a deep-drawn sigh) it is indeed, Sir.' 'Great Power, Sir' . . . 'Immense—immense!' 'Great deal done by steam, Sir.' 'Ah! (another sigh at the immensity of the subject, and a knowing shake of the head) you may say that, Sir.' 'Still in its infancy they say, Sir.' "[15] There is no social significance, only genial satire aimed at the petty foible of dull conversation. In the early writings, steam power is an excuse for a friendly chat, and technology an unobtrusive element in the traditional world of sunny excursions.

The Thames is also the center of action in *Our Mutual Friend,* but a happy pleasure trip downriver would be unthinkable in the dismal atmosphere of Dickens' last novel. The book's theme is the corrupting power of wealth; its plot concerns a fortune appropriately derived from London's dust heaps. The river here is a dark and oily stream in which men fish for dead bodies, and the single steamer that appears comes out of the fog to run down Rogue Riderhood. The river people comment that "it always *is* a steamer" that runs down innocent people; they call the fog-shrouded craft "Murderer, bound for Gallows Bay . . . Manslaughterer, bound for Penal Settlement."[16] Here the steamship has become a symbol of impersonal oppressive power, an emblem of the callous cruelty pervading Victorian life.

From *Pickwick* (1836) to *The Old Curiosity Shop* (1840-41), Dickens' England is primarily pastoral, a world in which machine technology, when it appears at all, is seen only as an alien, almost unintelligible phenomenon. In *Pickwick,* the factories, with their "lurid, sullen light,"[17] are curiosities lining the roads around Birmingham. Within the world of the stagecoach, the machine has little social effect and no symbolic importance.

To describe the unfamiliar mechanized landscape in *The Old Curiosity Shop,* Dickens again uses the technological sublime to evoke its fearfulness and unreality. To see the factory is to have a momentary glimpse into the inferno. In the satanic mills, men move "like demons among the flame and smoke."[18] Amidst the general disillusionment with industry in the economic decline of the 1830's and the 1840's, exemplified in this novel, there were many similar descriptions of manufacturing as a modern hell. Entering Manchester, Coningsby "passed over the plains where iron and coal supersede turf and corn, dingy as the entrance of Hades, and flaming with furnaces."[19] In one of her rare descriptions of a factory interior, Mrs. Gaskell writes: "In the furnace-house, a deep and lurid red glared over all; the furnace roared with mighty flame. The men, like demons, in their fire-and-soot coloring, stood swart around."[20] And a tour of the Black Country even inspired John Martin's illustrations of Pandemonium in *Paradise Lost.*[21]

But even in *The Old Curiosity Shop,* Dickens' use of the machine goes beyond the simple message that "work is Hell" to a new order of symbolic complexity.

The "strangest engines [that] spun and writhed like tortured creatures; clanking their iron chains, shrieking in their rapid whirl from time to time as though in torment unendurable, and making the ground tremble with their agonies," suggest the animal violence that he feared the suffering created by industrialism would arouse. The machines are the image of the Chartists, the ferocious men "armed with sword and fire-brand" who rushed forth on "errands of terror and destruction, to work no ruin half so surely as their own."[22] And yet, for all its social suggestiveness, the picture of the mechanized landscape is still primarily a stage-set against which is played a single trial in the life of little Nell. The machine is not integrated into the symbolic pattern of the book because it has not yet become part of Dickens' world. Though technology may form islands of horror within the countryside, a few days' walk takes Nell and her grandfather to the quiet kindness of pastoral England.

The machine first appears an integral part of daily life, and as such a symbol of forces controlling English society, in *Dombey and Son*. Although published in 1848, ten years after the early railway construction in London it describes, an intense interest in the railway, aroused by the extravagant railway speculation of the 1840's, runs through the work. As usual, in praising the machine, Dickens highlights the grotesque, the disordered, the unique, as in this description of the Camden Town railway excavation:

> The first shock of a great earthquake had, just at that period, rent the whole neighbourhood to its center . . . Houses were knocked down; streets broken through and

stopped; deep pits and trenches dug in the ground; enormous heaps of earth and clay thrown up; buildings that were undermined and shaking, propped by great beams of wood. Here, a chaos of carts, overthrown and jumbled together, lay topsy-turvey at the bottom of a steep unnatural hill; there, confused treasures of iron soaked and rusted in something that accidentally became a pond ... Boiling water hissed and heaved within dilapidated walls; whence, also, the glare and roar of flames came issuing forth; and mounds of ashes blocked up rights of way, and wholly changed the law and custom of the neighbourhood.[23]

Dickens was always inspired by the apparent jumble and confusion of technology. In picturing a railway junction in *The Lazy Tour of Two Idle Apprentices,* he dwells on the magnificence of its disorder: "All manner of cross-lines came zig-zagging into it, like a Congress of iron vipers; and, a little way out of it, a pointsman in an elevated signal box was constantly going through the motions of drawing immense quantities of beer at a public-house bar."[24] In "Mugby Junction" he singles out the "iron-barred cages full of cattle jangling by midway, the drooping beasts with horns entangled, eyes frozen with terror, and mouths too."[25] The regular and disciplined action of the machine, which was to be the basis of the modern machine aesthetic, fills Dickens with dread and characterizes only the engines in the soul-destroying world of *Hard Times.*

In *Dombey,* too, Dickens is able to capture the atmosphere of the machine age without including concrete technical details, a quality that characterizes all his writings on machinery. "A Poor Man's Tale of a

Patent," concerning a virtuous machinist's difficulties
in patenting an invention, is filled with details of the
legal process, but Dickens never names the new machine.
The protagonist merely says: "I have been twenty year,
off and on, completing an Invention and perfecting it.
I perfected of it, last Christmas Eve at ten o'clock at
night."[26] There is none of the pseudo-science that H. G.
Wells injects into similar accounts of scientists. And
yet it is symptomatic of Dickens' interest in technological development that, however vague the invention
might be, the moral of the story is that the patent laws
must be simplified to encourage progress.

Indifferent to the intricacies of technology, Dickens
sought to fix the effect of the machine age on the sensibility. His description of Dombey's train ride, for example, concentrates less on the details of steam locomotion and more on the sensations of the journey, such
as the optical illusions. Even the rhythm of the words is
aimed at conveying the new sensations of speed. "Away,
with a shriek, and a roar, and a rattle, through the fields,
through the woods, through the corn, through the hay,
through the chalk, through the mould, through the clay,
through the rock, among objects close at hand and
almost in the grasp, ever flying from the traveller, and a
deceitful distance ever moving slowly with him."[27]

Although the sense of technological change pervades the work, Dickens is less interested in its social
and even its psychological effects than in using the
machine as a symbol of the emotional and moral life of
his time. He divides the characters into two sets, each
gravitating toward a different center. The selfish

schemers, Major Bagstock, Carker, Mrs. Granger, find their way to Dombey's dark mansion where, beneath the mask of social respectability, they pander to his sin of pride. In the cozy instrument shop of Solomon Gills gather Florence, Captain Cuttle, and Walter Gay, all exemplifying the quality of spontaneous moral sympathy. These inhabitants of Gills's island of benevolence are outcasts from a mechanized England; their simple virtues are consistently associated with the ways of England before the machine. Earlier, the boys at Doctor Blimber's term Paul Dombey's childish sweetness "old fashioned."[28] Captain Cuttle, the reader is sure, has never set foot on a steamer. Sol Gills's handmade navigational devices can no longer compete with "new invention, new invention—alteration, alteration." He laments: "The world's gone past me, I hardly know myself; much less where my customers are."[29] The gentle Gills and the simple Cuttle, invisible in their fairy-tale nautical world enclosed by London's financial district, become, like little Nell and her grandfather in the Black Country, the emblems of intuitive morality threatened by a mechanized world.

Dombey himself is hardly a leader of the technological revolution. With the exception of Rouncewell, the ironmaster in *Bleak House* who exemplifies the Carlylean ideal of technologist as hero, industrialists seldom appear in Dickens' work. Dombey is a preindustrial businessman who operates, with Carker, a typically eighteenth-century concern, an export firm trading with the West Indies. Although Dombey and Carker are not representatives of the new technology, the machine still serves to symbolize their indifference and rapacity; for if Dickens associates intuitive benevolence with pastoral England, he connects its decline with technological progress. As Dombey rides the train to Leamington after the death of his son, bitter pride drives out generous grief. His jealous hatred, intensified by his broken hopes for perpetuating the firm, fastens on Florence and especially on Toodle, who has dared to share his mourning for Paul. The progress of the train over the landscape suggests not only the physical death of Paul Dombey but the death of feeling within Dombey himself.

> He found no pleasure or relief in the journey. Tortured by these thoughts he carried monotony with him, through the rushing landscape, and hurried headlong, not through a rich and varied country, but a wilderness of blighted plans and gnawing jealousies. The very speed at which the train was whirled along, mocked the swift course of the young life that had been borne away so steadily and inexorably to its fore-doomed end. The power that forced itself upon its iron way—its own—defiant of all paths and roads, piercing through the heart of every obstacle, and dragging living creatures of all classes, ages, and degrees behind it, was a type of the triumphant monster, Death . . .
>
> Away, with a shriek, and a roar, and a rattle and no trace to leave behind but dust and vapour: like as in the track of the remorseless monster, Death![30]

Here the railway becomes, like the "huge, dead" steam engine of *Sartor,* the emblem of philosophic necessity. Furthermore, the industrial wasteland through which the train runs is not merely an objective correlative for the emotional blight of Dombey's mind but suggests also in its destruction of an older way of life that the machine is in some way responsible for this emotional desiccation. With its simultaneous sense of philosophic determinism, social change, and emotional desolation, the train becomes a complex symbol of Victorian life. It finally reaches its destination in the industrialized city where "everything . . . is blackened."

And yet, even here Dickens' ambivalence to the machine works to tone down the attack on mechanization and thus vitiate the imaginative force of the whole. Toward the end of the description, his bourgeois enthusiasm asserts itself: "As Mr. Dombey looks out of his carriage window, it is never in his thoughts that the monster who has brought him there has let the light of day in on these things: not made or caused them."[31] It is as if Dickens suddenly remembered the material benefits of England's progress.

In spite of Dickens' occasional special pleading, the machine usually works in the novel to symbolize the union of economic power with moral indifference. This use becomes explicit in the words of Mr. Moffin, the typical Dickensian *deus ex machina,* kindly, elderly, unbelievably generous. In the uniformly grim world of *Dombey and Son,* however, such characters can no longer influence the central action; Mr. Moffin is relegated to a subplot as the savior of John Carker and his sister. Spontaneous benevolence requires no explanation, but Dickens illustrates Moffin's former sins of gentle, yet self-centered indifference with an image drawn from contemporary technology. Explaining his former failure to be of assistance, Moffin says: "[I was] quite content to be as little troubled as I might be, out of my own strip of duty, and to let everything about me go on, day by day, unquestioned, like a great machine —that was its habit and mine—and to take it all for granted, and consider it all right."[32] Moffin's indifference is a passive counterpart of Dombey and Carker's ruthless use of commercial power.

The machine becomes an agent in the plot as well as symbol only in the novel's climactic event, Carker's death under the wheels of the London express. For all its melodrama, the event rings true, truer than if, for example, Carker had been run down by a stagecoach, for Dickens' consistent symbolic association of the machine with amoral power has prepared the reader for the action. The train which carries Dombey tears ruthlessly through the landscape; it is fitting that Carker should meet his death from a machine which exemplifies his own destructive energies.

In the picture of Carker's last hours, Dickens has provided a penetrating psychological study. Enraged at his rejection by Edith and unnerved by his long journey, Carker can scarcely control his wish for self-destruction. He feels a strange kinship with the locomotives thundering by his hotel and is drawn out to look at one: "He stood parallel with it, watching its heavy wheels and brazen front, and thinking what a cruel power and might it had."[33] Perceiving in the machine the type of his own demonic energies, he can scarcely keep from then throwing himself beneath the wheels. Death when it comes is accidental, a startled fall into the path of the train on seeing Dombey; but in both the psychological and the symbolic sense it is suicide. The death of Carker beneath the machine that objectifies his own amoral power suggests, as does Dombey's train, the self-destructive energy of technological power uncontrolled by ethics.

Although the associations that cluster about the machine indicate the strength of Dickens' disillusionment with technology, the novel is scarcely a tract against the railway. Dickens' pride in progress kept him from constructing a neat symbolic pattern in which goodness withers as the machine advances. If he saw in the railway the image of cruelty, he also felt, like Coningsby entering Manchester,[34] the breath of romance that technology brought to Victorian life. He expresses his delight in the mechanized present through the character of Toodle. True, the path of the railway cuts through the jumble of Staggs's Gardens, obliterating Toodle's happy home, which Dickens contrasts with Dombey's somber mansion, and displacing his ebullient brood of children. Yet Dickens approves of the Victorian redevelopment scheme with as much pleasure as many an urban planner contemplates the destruction of Greenwich Village: "Where the old rotten summer-houses once had stood, palaces now reared their heads, and granite columns of gigantic girth opened a vista to the railway world beyond. The miserable waste ground, where the refuse-matter had been heaped of yore, was swallowed up and gone; and in its frowsy stead were tiers of warehouses, crammed with rich goods and costly merchandise."[35] The locomotives are celebrated as signs of man's control over natural forces, "gliding like tame dragons into the allotted corner grooved out to the inch for their reception . . . dilating with the secret knowledge of great powers yet unsuspected in them, and strong purposes not yet achieved."[36] The railway even provides the family with new housing and gives Toodle a job as locomotive fireman that is not only safer than his former work in the mines,[37] but also stirs his soul with the romance of machinery: "He was either taking refreshment in the bosom just mentioned [that is, of his family], or he was tearing through the country at from twenty-five to fifty miles an hour, or he was sleeping after his fatigues."[38] Although the railway molds his speech, his connection with the machine does not in any way warp his intuitive morality; he advises his children: "Wotever you're up to in a honest way, it's my opinion as you can't do better than be open. If you find yourselves in cuttings or in tunnels, don't you play no secret games. Keep your whistles going, and let's know where you are."[39]

Dickens could present Toodle's morality in railway terminology as easily as he could symbolize Carker's amorality in the locomotive because of his own ambivalence to the machine. Furthermore, if the machine takes on different symbolic values in this novel, it is because the work, unlike *Hard Times,* is not primarily concerned with mechanization as a reason for the failure of imaginative sympathy, but with an amoral commercialism for which the machine can serve as symbol. Ethical action in *Dombey and Son* does not depend upon social or technological change but upon an instinctive moral sense which, as Toodle demonstrates, is immune to the effects of technology.

ii

By 1854 Dickens' imagination had so absorbed the fact of England's mechanization that he could write a novel set wholly in an industrialized world. No longer is the mechanized landscape an excrescence on the surface of England, a setting through which characters such as little Nell and even Dombey pass on their way to their normal lives in the country or the countinghouse. In *Hard Times* the mechanized world has become the setting of daily life and the pastoral world a place of temporary refuge. As Rachel and Sissy refresh themselves with a short Sunday expedition, "in the distance one way, Coketown showed as a black mist; in another distance hills began to rise; in a third there was a faint change in the light of the horizon where it shone upon the far-off sea . . . Engines at pits' mouths, and lean old horses that had worn the circle of their daily labour into the ground, were alike quiet; wheels had ceased for a short space to turn; and the great wheel of earth seemed to revolve without the shocks and noises of another time."[40] In a society wholly mechanized, in which even the rotating earth is seen as a great iron flywheel, the machine becomes the symbol of English life as a whole, suggesting not only as in *Dombey* the decline of intuitive morality, and not only as in Carlyle the mechanistic assumptions justifying this amorality, but also the tangible psychological dangers created by mechanization itself. For here Coketown *is* England, and the machine the symbol of the combination of intellectual mechanism and industrial mechanization that Dickens sees dominating English life.

Hard Times has always been recognized as a curious sport among Dickens' novels. Although its themes are consistent with the rest of his work, its tone is strikingly different; for it has the virtually unrelieved grimness of a reforming tract, with little of the exuberance that creeps into even the darkest of the late novels. The bleakness is in part due to his lack of interest in the intricacies of industrial technology. Although he saw the factories of England and America at first hand, his imagination never thrilled to mechanized manufacturing as it did to the railway. At the mills of Lowell, Massachusetts, for example, he notes the factory girls' housing and their virtuous after-hours pursuits, but gives no descriptions of textile machinery to equal his detailed comparisons of English and American railways.[41] Furthermore, he felt himself a stranger upon the industrial scene. He had not lived among factories in his formative years but had moved amid the bustle of the London streets, and his descriptions of industrial workers, untouched by the emotional warmth of memory, are those of an outsider. And yet, this grayness of tone is perfectly suited to his theme. If Stephen and Rachel are dull, it is because of their dulling work and dulling environment. If Louisa and Tom do not seem to "live," it is because "living" has never been allowed. If Gradgrind is a caricature, it is because rigid doctrines repress his emotional life. And if Bounderby is the char-

acter most "alive" in the work, it is because he is neither
a utilitarian nor, in spite of his profession, a technologist, but, dining on venison and tyrannizing over his de-
pendents, an eighteenth-century squire untouched by
the mechanized world.

Like *Dombey, Hard Times* criticizes not a person,
but an emotional atmosphere, a state of mind symbolized by the machine. But whereas the earlier book considers the commercial mind that could flourish in an
eighteenth-century countinghouse, the latter lashes out
at a creed peculiar to the industrial age. Dickens is
specifically indicting the utilitarians, but more generally, he is attacking the mechanistic mode of thought
of which the Benthamite creed is one example. Within
the novel, plot and symbol are organized to indicate
the major theme of nineteenth- and twentieth-century
literature, the suppression of emotional impulse by the
false application of the machine metaphor. Even the
physical form of Coketown is seen as an extension of the
order of its factories: "It contained several large streets
all very like one another, and many small streets still
more like one another, inhabited by people equally like
one another, who all went in and out at the same
hours . . . If the members of a religious persuasion built
a chapel there . . . they made it a pious warehouse of
red brick, with sometimes (but this is only in highly
ornamental examples) a bell in a birdcage on the top of
it."[42] The Louisa-Harthouse plot and the industrial
strife are thematically connected in showing how rationalistic perfection stifles, and thus corrupts, natural

impulses. In the convention of the technological sublime, Dickens uses the industrial scene, as in *The Old
Curiosity Shop,* to mirror the eruption of this suppressed emotional energy. As her father presses her to
marry Bounderby, Louisa comments on Coketown in
a figure that applies simultaneously to her own stifled
passion and the resentment of the workers: "There
seems to be nothing there but languid and monotonous
smoke. Yet when the night comes, Fire bursts out,
father."[43]

Within the "town of machinery," the steam engine
is the primary symbol of the dangerous unnaturalness
of the disciplined life. Even the conventional anthropomorphic description is functional in suggesting the
draining of vitality from the worker into the machine.
In the factory, "the piston of the steam-engine worked
monotonously up and down like the head of an elephant
in a state of melancholy madness."[44] The important
word is "madness." Throughout the book the figure of
the stationary engine as a "mad" elephant emphasizes
that the ceaseless repetition of mechanized labor is an
aberration from normal emotional rhythms. The day
starts with "a clattering of clogs upon the pavement; a
rapid ringing of bells; and all of the melancholy mad
elephants polished and oiled up for the day's monotony,
were at their heavy exercise again."[45] The machine re-
peats its insane pattern heedless of its human attendants.
On hot summer days, the factory workers, "wasting with
heat, toiled languidly in the desert. But no temperature
made the melancholy mad elephants more mad or more

sane. Their wearisome heads went up and down at the same rate, in hot weather and cold, wet weather and dry, fair weather and foul."[46]

Most important to Dickens is the patterning of education on the metaphor of man as machine. Mr. M'Choakumchild, the new teacher at Mr. Gradgrind's school, is, like his employer, a well-meaning man. He is merely following the spirit of the age in applying to education the principle so successful in mechanized industry: standardized methods applied to standardized material produce maximum results. This application of industrial techniques to human material, seen by Dickens as well as Carlyle as a sign of the times, seemed to both not only erroneous but potentially dangerous. In "Signs of the Times," Carlyle had with heavy irony called the application of the division of labor to education "a secure, universal straightforward business to be conducted in the gross, by proper mechanism."[47] Dickens, too, draws heavily on the pejorative sense of the machine metaphor to criticize the new mass production of teachers: "He and some one hundred and forty other schoolmasters had been lately turned at the same time, in the same factory, on the same principles, like so many pianoforte legs."[48] With the emphasis in the teacher-training schools on rote memorization of set answers to the single national certificate examinations, the analogy of the factory is quite apt. Just as Mr. M'Choakumchild has been turned to inert matter by his mechanized education, so too the school will substitute the workings of the reason and memory for the spontaneous impulses of the imagination. For this unnatural and destructive process, Dickens uses a machine analogy as a further suggestion that mechanistic thought is as powerful, and as dangerous, as the machine itself. Gradgrind, standing before the children whom his system will destroy, is compared to a static-electricity machine, "a galvinizing apparatus . . . charged with a grim mechanical substitute for the tender young imaginations that were to be stormed away."[49]

The attack on the mechanization of the spirit in education is only one example of the Carlylean cast of the work. For Dickens succeeded in producing a fable illustrating Carlyle's attack on machinery in its "inward" and "outward" sense. Before the book appeared he had written to Carlyle: "It contains what I do devoutly hope will shake some people in a terrible mistake of these days . . . I know it contains nothing in which you do not think with me, for no man knows your books better than I. I want to put in the first page of it that it is inscribed to Thomas Carlyle."[50] To both men the "terrible mistake of these days" was intellectual mechanism, the philosophy that by considering men as soulless interchangeable parts reduced what Dickens called the "subtle essence of humanity"[51] to quantitative terms. Both trusted the mysterious promptings of intuition that followed neither rule nor self-interest. To each, then, the machine became both cause and symbol of the contemporary desire to impose on these spontaneous impulses of organic life the destructive exactness of scientific rationality and utilitarian organization. And yet each kept his faith that the intuitive self could never be reduced to the regularity so admired in machinery. So Dickens assured his readers in an apostrophe that, epitomizing Carlyle's thought, even takes on his diction:

> Never fear, good people of an anxious turn of mind, that Art will consign Nature to oblivion . . .
> So many hundred Hands in this Mill; so many hundred horse Steam Power. It is known, to the force of a single pound weight, what the engine will do; but, not all the calculators of the National Debt can tell me the capacity for good or evil, for love or hatred, for patriotism or discontent, for the decomposition of virtue into vice, or the reverse, at any single moment in the soul of one of these its quiet servants, with the composed faces and the regulated actions. There is no mystery in it; there is an unfathomable mystery in the meanest of them, for ever.[52]

The fallacy of considering the workers within the quantitative methods of science becomes the main point in his critique of Benthamite social theory. Stephen Blackpool, speaking for Dickens and echoing Carlyle, tells Bounderby that the root of the workers' discontent is not material but spiritual, not low wages but their sense of isolation:

> . . . rating 'em as so much Power, and reg'latin 'em as if they was figures in a soom, or machines: wi'out loves and likens, wi'out memories and inclinations, wi'out souls to weary and souls to hope—when aw goes quiet, draggin on wi' 'em as if they'd nowt o' th' kind, and when aw goes onquiet, reproaching 'em for their want of sitch humanly feelins in their dealins wi' yo—this will never do 't, sir, till God's work is onmade.[53]

Implicit in this set piece, and responsible for Dickens'

antipathy to the strikers, is the Carlylean position that industrial society should not be organized to run with the impersonality of a machine, but should create a new organic society growing out of emotional bonds of loyalty and respect.

But Carlyle's Calvinist delight in work had prevented him from fully realizing the emotional dangers of mechanized labor. Dickens, psychically scarred by his ordeal in the blacking warehouse, was far more sensitive to the influence of working conditions on the affective life. Throughout his writing and his efforts at practical reform, there runs a persistent concern with not only the physical but the emotional effects of machine-tending. As *Dombey* concentrates on the characters' emotional responses to the railway, so *Hard Times* focuses on the effect of mechanized labor on the workers' minds. Although the book never describes a factory interior, it abounds with attempts to describe the psychological state of a machine-tender. For example, he pictures the workers straining to concentrate in the turmoil of the factory after seeing the notice condemning Blackpool: "Many ears and eyes were busy with a vision of the matter of these placards, among turning spindles, rattling looms, and whirling wheels, for hours afterwards."[54] After work, Blackpool feels "the old sensation upon him which the stoppage of the machinery always produced—the sensation of its having worked and stopped in his own head."[55] Later, he dozes fitfully and "as he listened to the great noise of the wind, he ceased to hear it, or it changed into the working of his loom."[56] As the dream continues, his loom takes the shape of the justice that prevents him from acquiescing in his wife's death: "He stood on a raised stage, under his own loom; and, looking up at the shape the loom took, and hearing the burial service distinctly read, he knew that he was there to suffer death. In an instant what he stood on fell below him, and he was gone."[57] The mind has transformed the loom into a gallows.

This sense of the tangible psychological effects of machine-tending sets *Hard Times* apart from contemporaneous industrial novels. Most early Victorian descriptions of industrialism center on the physical suffering caused by mechanization. One of the sharpest pictures in Disraeli's *Sybil* is of the hand-loom weaver forced out of his traditional craft by the machine and unable to purchase food for his starving children. There is in *Sybil,* too, a Zolaesque description of human brutalization in the iron-workers of Wodgate, but Disraeli attributes their animality less to the nature of their work than to their isolation from the tempering effect of aristocratic gentility. Mrs. Gaskell, having lived in Manchester, was overwhelmed by the simple fact of starvation and disease; *North and South* and *Mary Barton* picture a hell of "clemming" children in filthy cellars, and advocate as remedies a personal charity and Carlylean paternalism. Of the reforming novelists, only Dickens, the master describer of urban squalor, saw the psychic harm caused by the mechanization of labor.

Long before he wrote *Hard Times,* Dickens had been actively concerned with the baneful psychological results of factory work. During the 1840's he traveled throughout the Midlands to raise money for educational facilities that factory workers could use in their scant leisure time. At Liverpool, at Manchester, at Birmingham, the point of his speeches was identical: machine-tending is an unnatural discipline destructive of beneficent natural impulses and as such must be counteracted by a nonscientific education. "It surely cannot be allowed that those who labour day by day, surrounded by machinery, shall be permitted to degenerate into machines themselves; but, on the contrary, they should be able to assert their common origin in that Creator from whose wondrous hands they come."[58] "Wherever hammers beat, or wherever factory chimneys smoke; wherever hands are busy, or the clanking of machinery resounds; wherever, in a word, there are masses of industrious beings whom their wise Creator did not see fit to constitute all body, but into each and every one of whom he breathed a mind,"[59] education in the arts, an increase in reading of imaginative literature is needed so that the orderly habits imposed on the mind by the "constant contemplation of the steam engine"[60] can be thrown off by a cultivation of the imagination. Implicit throughout his plans for the education of industrial workers is the romantic premise of an unbridgeable gap between the reason and feeling, between the facts of quantitative science and the insights of intuition: "Do not let us, in the midst of the visible objects of nature, whose workings we can tell off in figures, surrounded by machines that can be made to the thousandth part of an inch, acquiring every day knowledge which can be proved upon a slate or demonstrated by a microscope—do not let us, in the laudable pursuits of the facts that surround us, neglect the fancy and the imagination."[61]

Although Dickens' criticism of industrial discipline may sound familiar in the twentieth century, it was a radical notion in his day. Not only the manufacturers, but the middle-class public seemed to feel a complacent pride in the discipline mechanization imposed on the working class. Andrew Ure, a well-known apologist for industry, caught the spirit of the time in praising Arkwright not only for organizing the processes of manufacturing but also for "training human beings to renounce their desultory habits of work, and to identify themselves with the unvarying regularity of the complex automaton."[62] Even Mrs. Gaskell, for all the clarity of vision with which she sees the physical degradation of the industrial worker, praises his tenacity in matching the repetitive rhythms of the machine: "Senseless and purposeless were wood and iron and steam in their endless labours; but the persistence of their monotonous work was rivalled in tireless endurance by the strong crowds, who, with sense and with purpose, were busy and restless in seeking after— What?"[63]

Throughout *Hard Times*, Dickens attacks the regimentation of the emotions both inside and outside the factory by contrasting life ordered by the machine to that regulated by the rhythms of organic life. The horse riders work with animals, not spinning machines, and the novel suggests that it is this more "natural" work that accounts for their emotional strength. Because horse riding involves responsive animals rather than predictable machines, it demands the full play of both the body and the intuition, with only a minimal use of the rational mind that Dickens always distrusted. Such organic work develops people who are not only more lively but also more benevolent. Dickens based his criticism of mechanization not on any longing for the lost skill of the craftsman but on his belief that the deadening of the imagination must destroy the moral sense. The impulsive generosity of Sleary's troop is morally superior to the heartless rationality of Bitzer, the perfect product of Gradgrind's mechanistic education. As Dickens asserts explicitly in his speeches on education, only the cultivation of the feelings can lead to moral action: "If you would reward honesty, if you would give encouragement to good, if you would stimulate the ideal, eradicate evil, or correct what is bad, education—comprehensive liberal education—is the one thing needful, and the one effective end."[64]

In *Hard Times* the horse riders substitute for the workers' reading-rooms in arousing the suppressed fancy of the machine-tender and quickening the imagination of children formed on an educational assembly line. Their popularity testifies to the emotional needs unsatisfied by either mechanized work or a well-ordered environment. And yet the horse riders remain outsiders in the mechanized world. Their function is only to provide the Coketowners with a momentary escape into the imagination, in the same way that they themselves escape the reality of their poverty by donning the robes of nobility. Their way of life for all its spontaneous delight in work, its uncorrupted moral sense, its seeming freedom from economic necessity, is not taken as a serious alternative to mechanized society as it is, for example, in Morris' *News from Nowhere.* For although Dickens sensed the hazards of machine work, he was too loyal a member of the middle class ever to question the economic system that supported it. Ruskin's plan to control the machine by renouncing its products was to Dickens unthinkable. *Hard Times,* the finest imaginative account of the mechanized world in the nineteenth century, never calls for the elimination of, or restraints upon, the machine. Rachel returns to work.

Although Dickens is, in *Hard Times,* concerned with the effect of environment upon moral action, these effects here, as in other novels, are not exemplified in his main characters.[65] *Oliver Twist,* for example, may be meant to demonstrate how the poor laws incubate crime, yet Oliver emerges untainted from the poorhouse and Fagin's school. In writing of the mechanized world, too, Dickens always sought to show the staunchness of simple goodness rather than the dominance of harmful surroundings, the persistence of natural ethical impulse rather than the dulling moral effect of mechanized work. Although mechanized men appear in the background of his works, "demons among the flame and smoke"[66] in *The Old Curiosity Shop* and the gray mass of Coketown workers, the two fully described workers in *Hard Times* emerge uncorrupted from the regimentation of their lives. Besides some physical fatigue, fourteen hours at the loom does not seem to distort the moral sense of either Stephen or Rachel.

Because, unlike Ruskin, Dickens never questioned

the inevitability of mechanization and because, unlike
Carlyle, he always sought to counteract rather than
extend the regimentation demanded by the machine,
his hope for reform lay not so much in transforming
mechanized industry as in keeping feeling alive in a
mechanized world through liberal education and
through art. This belief, that the affective life could
survive the advance of the machine, becomes the central theme of his writings. I have already mentioned
Toodle, the engine fireman in *Dombey* whose compassion stands as a moral center within the novel. Toodle
takes on none of the qualities of the locomotive he
serves: "He was always in a whirlwind or a calm, and a
peaceable, contented, easy-going man Mr. Toodle was
in either state, who seemed to have made over all his
own inheritance of fuming and fretting to the engines
with which he was connected, which panted, and
gasped, and chafed, and wore themselves out, in a most
unsparing manner, while Mr. Toodle led a mild and
equable life."[67] His existence is not routinized nor his
imagination dulled by his contact with the machine.
With his verve and humorous gestures he seems more
the clown of the coaching yards than the efficient workman of the machine age.

In "Mugby Junction," one of his most popular
Christmas stories, Dickens creates another railway
worker who exemplifies the persistence of the imagination. The piece concerns a London bill-broker who ar-
rives in Mugby to escape the futility of his commercial
pursuits and forget his hatred of the wife who has
deserted him. His heart expands under the influence of

a cheerful crippled girl and her father, Lamps, whose job is checking the lights on trains that stop at the junction. Like Toodle, Lamps works with more gusto than efficiency, "skipping along the top of a train, from carriage to carriage, and catching lighted namesakes thrown up to him by a coadjutor."[68] His spirit has not acquired the regularity of the timetables, and the sight of "mysterious goods trains, covered with palls and gliding on like vast weird funerals,"[69] does not dim his cheerfulness. The imaginative power, which Dickens usually links to moral strength, survives in Lamps and overflows in the bad verse which he composes in off-duty moments. His daughter, of similar temperament, is also gladdened by the clatter and smoke of the distant trains. Eventually, the London man settles close to the warmhearted railway folk and when, on an expedition to the city, he encounters his wife, he forgives and aids her dying lover.

Among industrial machinery, too, unmechanized men survive. Even in the industrial inferno of *The Old Curiosity Shop,* one man has retained his moral impulses in spite of the Hellish conditions that have driven his fellow workers to madness. A young foundryman, the only fully characterized worker in the novel, acts with compassion in offering Nell and her grandfather a warm place by the furnace to sleep. Though the worker has spent his childhood in the foundry, the imagination from which his benevolence springs has flourished and, like the horse riders, he can escape from the scenes of industry into the realms of fancy. He gazes into the fire that he must feed and tells Nell: "It's like a book to me . . . the only book I ever learned to read; and many an old story it tells me. It's music, for I should know its voice among a thousand, and there are other voices in its roar. It has its pictures too. You don't know how many strange faces and different scenes I trace in the red-hot coals. It's my memory, that fire, and shows me all my life."[70]

This awareness that men are fated to coexist with the machine, but must ever work to preserve their emotional life from its deadening regularity, lies at the center of Dickens' work. Aware of the emotional price paid for the smooth functioning of a mechanized society, he nonetheless avoids both the authoritarianism of Carlyle's industrial armies and the unreality of Ruskin's pastoralism. He sought only what the inhabitants of a mechanized world can reasonably expect: "I often say to Mr. Gradgrind that there is reason and good intention in much that he does—but that he overdoes it. Perhaps by dint of his going his way and my going mine, we shall meet at last at some halfway house where there are flowers on the carpets, and a little standing-room for Queen Mab's chariot among the Steam Engines."[71]

Art and
3 the Machine:
John Ruskin

If the social and political changes created by the technological revolution were great, the transformation of the visible environment was no less thoroughgoing. The new machines themselves, the new structures built to serve their needs, the new methods of standardized production they made possible, all raised unprecedented aesthetic questions. Is a steam engine beautiful? What is the proper architectural style for a cotton mill? If the machine reproduces one thousand exactly similar carved piano-stools, is each a work of art? In dealing with these problems there arose in the nineteenth century two aesthetics. The first, the engineering style, describes the work of the builders of factories and railway bridges who, without an articulated theory, merely used the new technological means to do the job most efficiently. The exemplar of this style is Joseph Paxton, the designer of the Crystal Palace, who used standardized iron girders and glass panes because this method appeared to him the cheapest and fastest way to erect a large, temporary building. From this simple, efficient use of the machine, developed the spare functionalism of the modern machine aesthetic.[1]

But while the technologists were making the particular qualities of machine technology, standardization and strength of material, into the values of a new style, most Victorian writers on art were trying to counter the fact of mechanization by elevating opposing qualities, varied decoration and historical association, into aesthetic virtues. For this public style, for the anti-machine aesthetic of ornament and historicism, John Ruskin was both theoretician and spokesman. For all Ruskin's perception of the true nature of machine-art, his vitalistic assumptions about the natural world and the human psyche, the same romantic, antiscientific position exemplified in Dickens and in Ruskin's teacher Carlyle, made it impossible for him to accept the machine aesthetic. In a world properly understood as a living organism rather than as a giant steam engine, machines of iron failed in any way to imitate the beauty of God's world. And the factory worker, forced to imitate the regular rhythms of the machine, was made to follow an occupation equally unnatural. Seeing the machine as a tangible symbol of man's attempt to desecrate a sacramental world and machine production as an effort to destroy the analogue of God's power in the soul, Ruskin transformed the nineteenth-century dislike of the machine into a specifically moral crusade.

i

Beneath the contradictions and digressions spread out over sixty years and thirty-nine volumes of the

Library Edition, there run a few unchanging ideas which unify Ruskin's work. One is that the quality of art depends on the moral strength of the artist and thus, by implication, of the society to which the artist belongs. Another is the vitalistic, sacramental quality of the natural world. The antithetical influences of his youth, the poetry of Wordsworth and the evangelicalism of his mother, concurred on at least one point, that the visible world is but the embodiment of a transcendental power. As strongly as Carlyle, he rejected the Newtonian view of the world as inanimate objects moving in rigidly determined paths that could be predicted by the intellect and described by mathematics. In his autobiography, he could still remember the moment in the forest of Fontainebleau when he "felt upon his pulses" that the vital power moving in nature could be apprehended only through the vital power in his own soul rather than through the precise instruments of science:

> The woods, which I had only looked on as wilderness, fulfilled, I then saw, in their beauty, the same laws which guided the clouds, divided the light, and balanced the wave. "He hath made everything beautiful, in his time," became for me thenceforward the interpretation of the bond between the human mind and all visible things; and I returned along the wood-road feeling that it had led me far;—farther than ever fancy had reached, or theodolite measured.[2]

For Ruskin, the function of art is to imitate nature, but the application of this criterion depends, of course, on one's assumptions about nature. If, as Ruskin believed, nature is organic, ever varying in its manifestation of the vital energy within it, then art, to imitate nature, must, paradoxically, capture this "changefulness." The depiction in art of the specifically vitalistic quality of nature Ruskin calls "Organic Form" and, beneath the variations and digressions of his judgment, this criterion remains consistent: "The law which it has been my effort chiefly to illustrate is the dependence of all noble design, in any kind, on the sculpture or painting of Organic Form."[3] In analyzing "Water, as Painted by Turner," he praises Turner's accuracy in seeing the variation between the object and its reflection; for "nature contrives never to repeat herself, and the surface of water is not a mockery, but a new view of what is above it."[4] Or he praises Turner's painting of ocean waves for depicting the "sweeping exertion of tremendous and living strength."[5] Ruskin is not concerned as a cubist painter or a scientist might be in seeing the unchanging geometrical forms beneath the changing surface. His often-quoted statement that "a curve of any kind is more beautiful than a right line"[6] does not merely express an idiosyncrasy of temperament, but the fundamental principle that rectilinear forms are unnatural, distortions of the essentially curvilinear patterns and variations of a vitalistic nature.

It is the combination of this criterion of organic form, based on the rejection of the mechanistic world view, with his accurate perception of the proper qualities of a machine aesthetic that creates the seeming contradictions in Ruskin's discussion of the engineering style. For Ruskin consistently says, in statements that quoted out of context make him appear the apostle of modern design, that the machine in fulfilling its own unique nature will create wholly new aesthetic forms. He states, for example, that "the time is probably near when a new system of architectural laws will be developed, adapted entirely to metallic construction."[7] And he saw, too, that the combination of mathematics and machinery would quite properly turn out precise, geometrical objects; this spare functionalism even drew his grudging praise: "There is a meritorious finish . . . which fits a thing for its uses,—as a stone to lie well in its place, or a cog of an engine-wheel to play well on another."[8] But the irony is strong here; machine products may be "meritorious," but they are not art. For Ruskin, the machine aesthetic must be rejected because the machine, by its nature, is incapable of reproducing the irregularity and variety, the "Organic Form" of nature. "The moment the perceptions have been refined by reference to natural form, the eye requires perpetual variation and transgression of the formal law . . . But in good design all imitation by machinery is impossible. No curve is like another for an instant; no branch springs at an expected point."[9]

Ruskin was especially outraged at the use of the machine by Victorian designers to multiply naturalistic ornament. The crowds at the Crystal Palace thrilled at how easily the machine had re-created the variety of nature—in the silver bowls overgrown with silver vegetation applied by electroplating, in the furniture from which gutta-percha stags peered between gutta-percha leaves. But Ruskin was less impressed with the ingenuity of the new processes than with the unnaturalness of "all the stamped metals, and artificial stones, and imitation woods and bronzes, over the invention of which we hear daily exultation."[10]

But a case cannot be made for complete consistency in Ruskin. Sharing the ambivalence of most nineteenth-century writers, he was attracted by the power of the machine, and hoped to turn it to aesthetic uses, especially to the imitation of organic form. He suggests that

> the quaint beauty and character of many natural objects, such as intricate branches, grass, foliage . . . as well as that of many animals, plumed, spined, or bristled, is sculpturally expressible in iron only, and in iron would be majestic and impressive in the highest degree; and that every piece of metal work you use might be, rightly treated, not only a superb decoration, but a most valuable abstract of portions of natural forms.[11]

This urge to reconcile an older art imitating the surface of nature with the new technological methods was passed from Ruskin to his disciple William Morris, and through Morris to the art nouveau movement of the late nineteenth century. But the languid lampposts and wrought-iron foliage of art nouveau flourished only briefly, and the rapid demise of the style illustrates the truth of Ruskin's own basic principle that the machine is best suited to the production of standardized, geometrical forms.

For Ruskin, the ever varying forms of nature, inimitable by the regular repetitions of the machine, could only be captured by "the subtlest of all machines . . . the human hand. No machine yet contrived, or hereafter contrivable, will ever equal the fine machinery of the human fingers.''[12] This elevation of handwork as the sole method of true, which is to say imitative, art, taken out of context, had an enormous influence on the English arts and crafts movement and on uncounted thousands of suburban husbands. But for Ruskin the insistence on handwork is part of a more general defense of an essentially romantic aesthetic based on the idea of a vitalistic nature against a rationalized, scientific aesthetic he saw developing with technological progress. Beneath all his writings on art runs the assumption that the vital energy in nature has its analogue in a higher intuitive power that, capable of perceiving the transcendental, is capable of imitating organic form. For this ability to perceive "a more essential truth than is seen at the surface of things,''[13] Ruskin at the beginning of his writing used the conventional romantic name of the imagination; and though the terminology varied, his belief in art as the expression of a suprarational power never changed. Its effect is to make him consistently minimize the importance of intellect in art and architecture, to make him see reason as a lower faculty capable only of comprehending the causal relationships of the material world, as "the lower conditions of intellect which are concerned in the pursuit of natural science, or the invention of mechanical structure . . . [which] differ from the imaginative powers in that they are concerned with things seen—not with the evidences of things unseen.''[14] The process of creation is then defined in the irreconcilable opposites of the romantic aesthetic, the intuition as superior to the intellect, the intuitive perceptions of art superior to the dispassionate statements of science.[15] And thus Ruskin in applying the romantic aesthetic to the visual arts approaches the new machine aesthetic with the divided sensibility characteristic of his time. As Sigfried Giedion notes: "In the nineteenth century the paths of science and the arts diverged; the connection between methods of thinking and methods of feeling was broken. The mutual isolation of these two kinds of enterprise, far from being a consequence of their different natures, is a phenomenon peculiar to the nineteenth century."[16]

Nowhere is the distorting effect of the romantic antithesis between emotion and intellect more clearly demonstrated than in Ruskin's curious, yet quite consistent rejection of the engineering style in architecture. Aware of architecture as a reflection of society, he saw the great bridges and factories as signs of the times, as clear a manifestation of the technological ability of the nineteenth century as the gothic cathedrals are of the religious faith of the twelfth. "There is assuredly as much ingenuity required to build a screw frigate, or a tubular bridge, as a hall of glass;—all these are works characteristic of the age."[17] And yet he could not admire them as such. For to him the work of construction, no matter how skillful, no matter how functionally perfect, was still merely a product of the intellect; he calls it "building," a necessary but low grade skill involving the "animal faculties, an intricate bestiality."[18] Confident of the superiority of the imagination, he, like Carlyle, attributes technological progress solely to intuition. In the age of the engineer, he still thinks of the architect as

planning "not . . . with less instinct than the beaver or
the bee, but with more—with an innate cunning of proportion that embraces all beauty, and a divine ingenuity
of skill that improvises all construction."[19]

To re-create architecture that truly expresses intuitive powers, Ruskin looked to the Gothic style. Here
was a style whose essence is organicism, its twisting
acanthus leaves and grotesque animals attempts to capture organic form, its decorated surface an expression
of the felt religion of its sculptor, its "Savageness,"
"Changefulness," "Naturalism," "Grotesqueness," "Ri-
gidity," "Redundance,"[20] just those variable, imper-
fect qualities that the machine could not duplicate.
Furthermore, his entire conception of Gothic implies
no reconciliation of intellect and imagination in its
belief that a building is merely a canvas erected by the
reason for the purpose of being ornamented by the
imagination. But what he failed to realize is that the
religious spirit of a Gothic cathedral is expressed as
much through the spires built with the most advanced
contemporary technology as through the sculptured
forms of the surface.

If his equation of art with intuition and beauty
with organic form kept Ruskin not from perceiving but
from accepting the emerging machine aesthetic, his
romantic assumptions in combination with his evangelicalism did lead him to expand the modern awareness
of mechanization by transforming the common nineteenth-century sense of machine work as unnatural into
the assertion that it is immoral. His complex fusion of
the psychological dangers, the aesthetic faults, and the

social sinfulness implicit in the routinization of work first appears in "The Nature of Gothic," the most influential nineteenth-century discussion of the machine. Here he rejects geometrical forms, not only because they are not "true" to nature, but because their production inevitably suppresses free expression by the worker. In his historical argument, the carvers of Greek and Assyrian decoration were slaves because their work involved reproducing "mere geometrical forms—balls, ridges, and perfectly symmetrical foliage—which could be executed with absolute precision by line and rule."[21] He saw that in his own day the factory worker, occupied in producing standardized objects, is equally a slave in being forced to follow the regular and repetitive patterns of the machine. The metaphorical implications of his descriptions of the modern, routinized worker, like those of Dickens' image of the mechanized world in "melancholy mad elephants," stress the abnormality, the distortion of natural activity:

> Glass beads are utterly unnecessary, and there is no design or thought employed in their manufacture. They are formed by first drawing out the glass into rods; these rods are chopped up into fragments of the size of beads by the human hand, and the fragments are then rounded in the furnace. The men who chop up the rods sit at their work all day, their hands vibrating with a perpetual and exquisitely timed palsy, and the beads dropping beneath their vibration like hail.[22]

But this routinized work is for Ruskin not only aberrant, it is sinful. And the fashionable young lady demanding these beads no matter what the cost to the producer, as representative of an acquisitive society, is engaging in an act of social sinfulness comparable to that epitome of social sin to the evangelical mind, the slave trade: "Every young lady, therefore, who buys glass beads is engaged in the slave-trade, and in a much more cruel one than that which we have so long been endeavouring to put down."[23] Allowing freedom of artistic expression, the prerequisite for creating organic form, then implies a moral position, a Christian recognition of the worth of each soul. Gothic appealed not only to Ruskin's eye but to his morality because its roughness symbolized the Christian belief that each man's work, from the grand design of the architect to the rudest carving of the stonecutter, is infinitely valuable in the sight of God.

If Ruskin could see the moral failure of the mechanized factory in which "the animation of her multitudes is sent like fuel to feed the factory smoke, and the strength of them is given daily to be wasted into the fineness of a web, or racked into the exactness of a line,"[24] he could not see that the repetitive function could be taken by the machine itself, and creativity exercised by the industrial designer who sets the pattern for the machine by a combination of intellect and imagination for which there is no word in Ruskin's vocabulary. Unable to accept regular geometrical forms as art, Ruskin took as his criteria for decorative art and architecture just those qualities that the machine cannot imitate—irregularity, variety, roughness. Seeking a public style in a world of more and more efficient machinery, Ruskin looks to an historicism that rejects the new economy, new efficiency, and new aesthetic values made possible by machine technology.

ii

The essential unity of Ruskin's vision, his complex sense of the interrelationship of mechanization, aesthetic failure, social sinfulness, and scientific thought, for which there are no abstract words in the language, is expressed in his writing through the symbol of the machine. For Ruskin, as for Carlyle, the single principle creating England's aesthetic, social, and psychological difficulties was the false application of the machine metaphor to organic processes. In his first explicit discussion of political and economic theory, *Unto This Last,* he shows how closely Benthamite thinking parallels the rationalizing of production in mechanized industry; the Benthamite, like the industrialist, applies quantitative criteria to the irregular rhythms of men, saying, according to Ruskin: "Let us eliminate the inconstants, and, considering the human being merely as a covetous machine, examine by what laws of labour, purchase, and sale, the greatest accumulative result in wealth is obtainable. Those laws once determined, it will be for each individual afterwards to introduce as much of the disturbing affectionate elements as he chooses, and to determine for himself the result on the new conditions supposed."[25] For Ruskin, the machine analogy fails because the "disturbing affectionate elements" are just those that distinguish organic life from inanimate matter, and building a science of behavior on causal predictability is like, in Ruskin's analogy, building a science of gymnastics on the assumption that men have no skeletons. The result is expressed in the common nineteenth-century figure of living matter physically distorted by mechanistic system: "It might be shown, on that supposition, that it would be advantageous to roll the students up into pellets, flatten them into cakes, or stretch them into cables; and that when these results were effected, the re-insertion of the skeleton would be attended with various inconveniences to their constitution. The reasoning might be admirable, the conclusions true, and the science deficient only in applicability."[26]

For the conceptual model of mechanism, Ruskin substitutes organic metaphors, often finding them, as Carlyle does, in the paradoxical figure of the vitalistic machine. Ruskin's quarrel is with the assumption of mechanistic science that if we but had enough information, organic activity would be wholly predictable; like Carlyle and Dickens, he makes the distinguishing quality of human life its mysterious freedom from determinism. Taking the example of the domestic servant, one of the few relationships remaining outside the cash-nexus in England, he says that the servant cannot be compared to an inanimate machine, "an engine of which the motive power was steam, magnetism, gravitation, or any other agent of calculable force."[27] He is, rather, a vitalistic machine, mysterious, intuitive, unpredictable; he is

an engine whose motive power is a Soul, the force of this very peculiar agent, as an unknown quantity, enters into all the political economist's equations, without his knowledge, and falsifies every one of their results. The largest quantity of work will not be done by this curious engine for pay, or under pressure, or by help of any kind of fuel which may be supplied by the chaldron. It will be done only when the motive force, that is to say, the will or spirit of the creature, is brought to its greatest strength by its own proper fuel: namely, by the affections.[28]

This opposition between the mechanistic and the organic becomes the defining distinction in the central occupation of Ruskin's social criticism, the redefinition of wealth. For the definition of wealth is, as Ruskin indicates, essentially a moral question, a choice of what is most valuable. And that which is most valuable Ruskin finds not in the ugly, useless items spawned with such ease by the machine; for these artifacts of mechanization, the opposite of true wealth, he coins the word "illth." True wealth is defined not as what the machine produces, but as what is natural, what is organic. "THERE IS," says Ruskin with capital letters to emphasize its centrality, "NO WEALTH BUT LIFE."[29] By "LIFE" he means not the passive satiation of the consumer, but the intense, integrated activity of physical strength and imaginative energy: "Labour is the contest of the life of man with an opposite;—the term 'life' including his intellect, soul, and physical power, contending with question, difficulty, trial, or material force."[30] It is this integrated activity that is being destroyed by the mechanization of labor. And life is, too, he says in *Fors*,[31] the direct enjoyment of the natural world—of hot sun, clear air, wholesome food, just those simple

sensual delights no longer possible in a blackened countryside.

In its redefinition of wealth, *Unto This Last* marks
a major transformation in the Victorian literary response to the machine. Carlyle, as a member of the first
generation in England to confront the machine, for all
his opposition to the combination of scientific thought
and social dislocation, could still envision psychological
and spiritual satisfaction in a paternalistic industrial
system. But, for all its indebtedness to Carlylean ideas,
Unto This Last articulates what had only been implicit
in earlier writings. It expresses the central paradox of
modern society, that as the machine advances, life, especially the inner life, becomes less satisfying, that by
its very nature the machine is destructive of those organic activities, creativity and physical well-being, which
are most valuable. This shift in emphasis, from machine
as servant of man to machine as destroyer of life, seems
to have occurred within literature during the 1850's.
Hard Times, in which the central metaphor is the conflict between mechanized and organic life, was written
during the same years that Ruskin was finishing "The
Nature of Gothic" and developing the ideas of *Unto
This Last.*[32] And in *Unto This Last,* Ruskin praises
Hard Times for the "wit and insight" in considering a
"subject of high national importance."[33] In 1850 Carlyle
published *Latter-Day Pamphlets.* In 1854 William Morris was reading "The Nature of Gothic" aloud to his
friends in his rooms at Oxford. By the 1850's, the railway, the most visible sign of technological change, had
after twenty years become commonplace, and the richer

life it and mechanized industry had promised had not come to pass. For literature, then, the decade of the Great Exhibition marks the end of hope in the blessings of the machine. To most writers it now appeared that the fact of technological power amidst physical and emotional poverty was not a temporary stop along the "ringing grooves" leading to a mechanized utopia, but an intransigent condition of modern life.

Ruskin's writings possess their greatest energy in discussing the intangible effect of the appearance of the mechanized world on the affective life. Although supremely sensitive to the ugliness of the industrial landscape, Ruskin was never concerned with appearance *per se.* Just as in *Modern Painters II* he sees "Aesthesis," "the mere animal consciousness of the pleasantness,"[34] as inferior to "Theoria," "the full comprehension and contemplation of the Beautiful as a gift of God,"[35] so too in describing the mechanized landscape he is less occupied with its visible appearance than with the physical fact as a sign of social immorality, and, conversely, with visual impression as a reason for this moral decline. In a lecture of 1859 on "Modern Manufacture and Design," he describes the visual quality of the mechanized environment through the familiar device of contrasts, comparing the "bright river . . . and brighter palaces" of Pisa with their "long successions of white pillars among wreaths of vine; leaping of fountains through buds of pomegranate and orange"[36] to the industrial landscape in which all organic life has been destroyed:

> The garden, blighted utterly into a field of ashes, not even a weed taking root there; the roof torn into shape-

less rents; the shutters hanging about the windows in
rags of rotten wood; before its gate, the stream which
had gladdened it now soaking slowly by, black as ebony
and thick with curdling scum; the bank above it trod-
den into unctuous, sooty slime: far in front of it, between it and the old hills, the furnaces of the city
foaming forth perpetual plague of sulphurous darkness;
the volumes of their storm clouds coiling low over a
waste of grassless fields.[37]

In the context, landscape is important not in itself,
but for its effect on the inner life in making impossible
that combination of visual sensitivity and moral energy
he saw as the prerequisite for art:

To men surrounded by the depressing and monotonous circumstances of English manufacturing life,
depend upon it, design is simply impossible . . . All the
lecturings, and teachings, and prizes, and principles of
art, in the world, are of no use, so long as you don't
surround your men with happy influences and beautiful
things. It is impossible for them to have right ideas
about colour, unless they see the lovely colours of
nature unspoiled; impossible for them to supply
beautiful incident and action in their ornament, unless
they see beautiful incident and action in the world
about them. Inform their minds, refine their habits, and
you form and refine their designs; but keep them
illiterate, uncomfortable, and in the midst of unbeauti-
ful things, and whatever they do will still be spurious,
vulgar, and valueless.[38]

The more specifically moral effects of the visual
environment are explored in the brilliant, mad essay,
"Fiction, Fair and Foul." Here in the industrial city,
inhabited by "children of to-day, accustomed, from the

instant they are out of their cradles, to the sight of this infinite nastiness, prevailing as a fixed condition of the universe," moral hope disappears, and men are left, as Carlyle had predicted in "Signs of the Times," with only the amoral activity of mechanistic science, with "the thrill of scientific vanity in the primary analysis of some unheard-of process of corruption—or the reward of microscopic research in the sight of worms with more legs, and acari of more curious generation than ever vivified the more simply smelling plasma of antiquity."[39]

His visual sensitivity, nourished by many leisurely family stagecoach trips, made him especially scornful of the Victorian delight in the speed made possible by the new technology. For he knew that the faster you go, the less you see: "There was always more in the world than men could see, walked they ever so slowly; they will see it no better for going fast . . . We shall be obliged at last to confess, what we should long ago have known, that the really precious things are thought and sight, not pace."[40] In his writings, as in Matthew Arnold's, demand for mechanized speed becomes one more example of the contemporary obsession with technological means rather than spiritual ends. In opposing "machinery" to culture, Arnold says: "Your middle-class man thinks it the highest pitch of development and civilisation when his letters are carried twelve times a day from Islington to Camberwell, and from Camberwell to Islington, and if railway trains run to and fro between them every quarter of an hour. He thinks it nothing that the trains only carry him from an illiberal, dismal life at Islington to an illiberal, dismal life at Camberwell."[41] Ruskin asks a similar question: "Telegraph signalling was a discovery; and conceivably, some day, may be a useful one . . . You knotted a copper wire all the way to Bombay, and flashed a message along it, and back. But what was the message, and what the answer? Is India the better for what you said to her? Are you the better for what she replied?"[42] Ruskin and Arnold are here both judging society by the criterion of whether it makes possible a rich inner life, but Ruskin is being far more primitivistic in equating value with the spontaneous activity of work destroyed by mechanization rather than as does Arnold, with the educated sensibility only tangentially affected by the machine.[43]

And yet, the irreconcilability Ruskin sees between the affective life and the machine leads to the impracticality of his social reforms. Since work still seemed to him a moral necessity, and kept by his ideas of organic form from accepting the machine aesthetic, he was forced inevitably into advocating handwork and simple physical toil. His obsession with useful work was quite as strong as Carlyle's and, like his teacher's, implanted by his Calvinist heritage. By losing himself in the creation of lines and colors, in stone-breaking for the road near Oxford, in sweeping a London street-crossing, he forgot for the moment the nagging guilt that abstract theorizing and the sensuous pleasures of art were not only useless but obscurely sinful. In *Fors* he cries out: "I am so alone now in my thoughts and ways, that if I am not mad, I should soon become so, from mere solitude, but for my *work*. But it must be manual work. Whenever I succeed in a drawing, I am happy, in spite of all that surrounds me of sorrow."[44]

Because he himself drew emotional strength from physical labor, he was almost totally oblivious to the value of technology in reducing the exhausting manual labor that is as emotionally destructive as the repetitive rhythm of the machine. H. G. Wells fills *A Modern Utopia* with such labor-saving devices as self-cleaning rooms; Ruskin remembers with delight washing the stairs of a Savoy inn:

> Nobody in the inn appearing to think it possible to wash it, I brought the necessary buckets of water from the yard myself, poured them into beautiful image of Versailles waterworks down the fifteen or twenty steps of the great staircase, and with the strongest broom I could find, cleaned every step into its corners. It was quite lovely work to dash the water and drive the mud, from each, with accumulating splash down to the next one.[45]

Although such occasional fits of labor were delightful to Ruskin, such work was appreciably less enjoyable, for example, to the charwomen who cleaned the steps after the Ruskin family had driven off. In his utopian vision, men earn their way by physical labor at such incontrovertibly useful occupations as farming. The Companions of St. George must swear, "I will labour, with such strength and opportunity as God gives me, for my own daily bread; and all that my hand finds to do, I will do with my might."[46] Such productive labor becomes a ransom for the idle afternoons spent cultivating the sensibility. He tells members of St. George's Company "not that they should abjure machinery . . . [but] that they should never do with a machine what can be done with hands and arms, while hands and arms are idle."[47]

The phrase "while hands and arms are idle" indicates the impetus that technological unemployment gave to Ruskin's desire to replace mechanized by manual labor. Imbued with the doctrine of work, Ruskin's revulsion at the sight of idle men, whether loungers in the Piazza San Marco or transient Irish labor in England, equaled Carlyle's. But whereas Carlyle envisioned mechanized industry as eventually providing the sacrament of work for the entire nation, Ruskin could only see the machine as eliminating jobs. In *The Crown of Wild Olive,* he takes the hypothetical example of a farmer employing one hundred men who buys a machine that can do the work of fifty. According to Ruskin the fifty displaced workers would either go on the dole or be forced into such frivolous occupations as making jewelry. To his evangelical sensibility, any work beyond the immediately productive was tinged with the sin of vanity and adequately covered by the heading of jewelry-making. With this narrow definition of useful activity, Ruskin could see the service occupations into which mechanization inevitably drove the worker only as the sinful pursuit of worldly pleasure. Far removed from the life of Coketown, or even from a real farm, Ruskin could not see that the machine is capable of freeing man from wearing physical toil. The moral of his parable is that the farmer should place ethics over eco-

nomics and, by scrapping the machine, restore the
workers to the satisfaction of physical labor.

The machine, then, for Ruskin is destructive only
when it interferes with the natural processes of muscular
activity and creative expression, where, to quote the
manifesto of St. George's Company, "it supersedes
healthy bodily exercise, or the art and precision of manual labour in decorative work."[48] But for tasks beyond
individual human strength, Ruskin saw no objection to
using the machine and, as fascinated as any Victorian
with the power of the new technology, he suggests
schemes that would do credit to H.G. Wells. He dreamed
of such "uses of machinery on a colossal scale . . . as the
deepening of large river channels;—changing the surface
of mountainous districts;—irrigating tracts of desert in
the torrid zone;—breaking up, and thus rendering capable of quicker fusion, edges of ice in the northern and
southern Arctic seas, etc., so rendering parts of the earth
habitable which hitherto have been lifeless."[49] Here, as
throughout his writing, the machine is a means of producing "wealth" in the most natural of occupations,
farming. And for all his visionary technological plans, his
purpose is never to create an industrial society but to
expand the traditional agricultural order.

Even in the territory of St. George, it is not the
machine itself, but only steam that is forbidden; for his
aim is not so much to exile technology as to banish ugliness. Steam can only be used outside the pastoral pre-
cincts of St. George and solely "under extreme or special
conditions of need; as for speed on main lines of communication."[50] His intense, almost physical aversion to

the sooty uncleanliness of the steam age made him dream of a new technology of clean, or as he called them, using the mechanistic-organic antithesis, "natural"[51] sources of power: "For all mechanical effort required in social life and in cities, water power is infinitely more than enough; for anchored mills on the large rivers, and mills moved by sluices from reservoirs filled by the tide, will give you command of any quantity of constant motive power you need."[52] The power of wind, and even of electricity met his approval because they too were smokeless.[53] This detestation of the sheer ugliness of steampowered technology, a reaction reinforced by the awareness of its destructive psychological effect, has been passed down through such disciples as William Morris to become part of the modern consciousness. Industry no longer wholly disregards aesthetic criteria, and the best architects use the new technology to make homes and even factories blend into, rather than despoil, the natural setting.[54]

But Ruskin could not reconcile himself even to an aesthetically pleasing industrial society because his values remained firmly grounded in the pastoral myth. First seen on his youthful visits with his father to the noble homes and parks of a country aristocracy and with the psychological necessity that makes the unattainable grow steadily more attractive, the vision of England as a garden grew greener as England grew blacker. He longed to ship mechanized industry off to the colonies and make England once more "the centre of the learning, of the arts, of the courtesies and felicities of the world . . . [to] cover her mountains with pasture; her plains with corn, her valleys with the lily, and her gardens with the rose."[55] In this vision of Arcadian perfection, the machine could have no place. With heavy humor he parodies "L'Allegro" to demonstrate the antithesis between the machine and the pastoral world:

> When young and old come forth to play
> On a sulphurous holiday,
> Tell how the darkling goblin sweat
> (His feast of cinders duly set),
> And belching night, where breathed the morn,
> His shadowy flail hath threshed the corn
> That ten day-labourers could not end.[56]

Milton's conventional landscape where "the milkmaid singeth blithe/And the mower whets his scythe" is far closer to Ruskin's ideal. But what Ruskin needed was a new version of Poussin's painting in which shepherds gaze at a steam engine on which is written *Et in Arcadia ego.* For in Ruskin's England, technological progress could not be rolled back, and because he rejected the very idea of a mechanized society, he forfeited any possibility of using the machine to expand the range of aesthetic and emotional experience. Instead, in his practical political writings and his unsuccessful efforts in St. George's Company, he found himself trying, with little success, to hold a few pastoral enclaves in an alien, mechanized land.

iii

But with Ruskin, to emphasize the fundamental intellectual unity in his response to the machine is to distort the tone of his writing. For his discussions of technology are not only quite disorganized but often quite absurd. There are such estimations of technological achievement as, "the great mechanical impulses of the age, of which most of us are so proud, are a mere passing fever, half-speculative, half-childish."[57] Furthermore, from the 1860's onward the descriptions of the machine are colored increasingly by his growing madness. And yet it is just this often clear-sighted madness that enables him to transcend the typical Victorian use of the machine as direct emblem of certain economic and intellectual qualities of the time. In his later writings, the machine is turned into an almost mystical symbol of a demonic evil spreading over English life and is set within an apocalyptic poetic vision that is comparable only to William Blake's. In these late writings, mechanization appears not merely as a specific, remediable social and aesthetic evil but as the manifestation of the principle of evil itself, as the same devil with whom he grappled in his fits of madness.[58] In *Fors* he advises a manufacturer to destroy his steam engine because, although "under certain limited needs, you may light fire, or use a fan, or distil water . . . to live by Fire is diabolical."[59] Like the devil, the machine has for Ruskin the strange attractiveness of evil, an evil that is consistently described as an aberration from God's natural order through comparisons to creatures traditionally considered abhorrent: "I cannot but more and more reverence the fierce courage and industry, the gloomy endurance, and the infinite mechanical ingenuity of the great centres [of manufacturing] as one reverences the fervid labours of a wasp's nest, though the end of all is only a noxious lump of clay."[60] Again and again, this fearful wonder at technological power is, in Ruskin's own version of the technological sublime, coupled with the figurative suggestion of the machine as incarnation of the evil principle:

> I sometimes watch a locomotive take its breath at a railway station, and think what work there is in its bars and wheels, and what manner of men they must be who dig brown iron-stone out of the ground, and forge it into THAT! What assemblage of accurate and mighty faculties in them; more than fleshly power over melting crag and coiling fire, fettered, and finessed at last into the precision of watchmaking; Titanian hammer-strokes beating . . . these glittering cylinders and timely-respondent valves, and fine ribbed rods, which touch each other as a serpent writhes, in noiseless gliding, and omnipotence of grasp; infinitely complex anatomy of active steel, compared with which the skeleton of a living creature would seem, to a careless observer, clumsy and vile.[61]

But, this Carlylean celebration of machinery in vitalistic terms is turned by the comparison of the driving rods to writhing serpents, the traditional guise of the devil. The description continues, using another creature to suggest the perverse evil of the machine: "But as I reach this point of reverence, the unreasonable thing is sure to give a shriek as of a thousand unanimous vultures, which leaves me shuddering in real physical pain for some half minute following."[62]

It is in the description of the industrialized landscape that Ruskin's poetic vision is most compelling.

His pictures of the mechanized world before the 1860's are still "realistic" social description, but in the 1860's and after, the fact of the machine becomes transmuted into a symbol within Ruskin's overriding vision of a world in which the sacramental natural order has been inverted and desecrated by the machine. If, as a recent critic has convincingly argued, in the "Storm Cloud of the Nineteenth Century" Ruskin is describing an actual darkening of the atmosphere after decades of industrial pollution,[63] the physical fact is transformed not merely into a sign of commercial self-interest but into a symbol of the fall of the modern world from God's grace:

> Blanched Sun,—blighted grass—blinded man. If, in conclusion, you ask me for any conceivable cause or meaning of these things—I can tell you none, according to your modern beliefs; but I can tell you what meaning it would have borne to the men of old time. Remember, for the last twenty years, England, and all foreign nations, either tempting her, or following her, have blasphemed the name of God deliberately and openly; and have done iniquity by proclamation, every man doing as much injustice to his brother as it is in his power to do.[64]

In *Fors* he inveighs against the pollution of the air—the "horrible nests, which you call towns, are little more than laboratories for the distillation into heaven of venomous smokes and smells, mixed with effluvia from decaying animal matter, and infectious miasmata from purulent disease"[65]—and of the water, but again the social fact is transformed into a religious symbol, the sign of a world given over to the devil and in which even the sacraments have been desecrated:

You might have the rivers of England as pure as the crystal of the rock; beautiful in falls, in lakes, in living pools; so full of fish that you might take them out with your hands instead of nets. Or you may do always as you have done now, turn every river of England into a common sewer, so that you cannot so much as baptize an English baby but with filth, unless you hold its face out in the rain; and even that falls dirty.[66]

Throughout these last works, his descriptions of the industrial scene become transcendental symbols of an evil principle manifested in a mechanized world in which organic life can no longer grow, in which the beauty of God's creation is fouled, in which the children have taken on the black, evil color of their environment, and in which, as in a Black Mass, the sacraments are mocked by a god of evil:

Children rolling on the heaps of black and slimy ground, mixed with brickbats and broken plates and bottles, in the midst of Preston or Wigan . . . the children themselves, black, and in rags evermore, and the only water near them either boiling, or gathered in unctuous pools, covered with rancid clots of scum . . . Are they not what your machine gods have produced for you?[67]

4   The Production of Art in the Machine Age: *William Morris*

To most Victorians, William Morris seemed a poet who had happened to take up the avocations of pattern-designing, interior decoration and, most curious of all, revolutionary socialism. And yet through these seemingly contradictory interests—escapist poetry, medieval handicraft, commercial success, socialism—there runs a single purpose; all are different means to the same end of freeing natural, organic impulses from the psychic restraints created by mechanization. The displacement of handwork by the machine becomes for Morris, as it does for Ruskin, but a specific example of the more general psychological dangers created by the combination of mechanization and mechanistic thought. And his writing transcends the mere defense of handicraft to become one of the most radical critiques of society in the nineteenth century, a plea for the use of machinery, not to increase production, but to make possible the free play of sensual, particularly sexual, energy.

i

All the influences of Morris' youth combined in turning him toward the traditional past rather than the mechanized future. His upper-middle-class family life was quite typically Victorian in looking down on the faintly vulgar technological progress that had created its wealth. William Morris, Sr., a discount broker who had made a lucky investment in a copper mine, raised his children in "an atmosphere of intelligent housekeeping of the old style—home-made beer and bread, real butter and real cream and the like."[1] The young boy feasted on Walter Scott and *The Arabian Nights* and took to roaming in the still primitive Epping Forest nearby. The rather casual classical education of his public school did little but give him time to indulge his delight in visiting Gothic churches and ancient ruins. By the time Morris entered Oxford in 1853, this nostalgic medievalism had crystallized into the desire to take High Church orders.

But Morris arrived at Oxford a few years too late. Newman's defection to Rome had wilted Oxford's brief religious renaissance, and Morris found himself seeking another outlet for his idealism. He soon fell in with a group of equally high-minded and directionless students that included his future associate, Edward Burne-Jones. The friends called themselves "The Brotherhood" and, having rejected clerical careers, envisioned such secular schemes as founding a nonreligious monastery to aid the poor. But before leaving Oxford, Morris found another way to combine idealism with worldly purpose, a new religion to replace the old in the doctrine of art as preached by John Ruskin. In sessions led by Morris who "chanted rather than read those weltering oceans of eloquence,"[2] the Brotherhood pored over the new volumes of *The Stones of Venice* as, in Morris' words, "a sort of revelation."[3] His tribute to Ruskin in the introduction to the Kelmscott edition of "The Nature of Gothic" suggests the formative effect of these pages on the lives of these idealistic young men: "To some of us when we first read it, now many years ago, it seemed to point out a new road on which the world should travel."[4]

Throughout his writings, especially in his conception of mechanized work and of the relation between this work and ethical values, Morris remained a Ruskinian. He agreed with Ruskin's basic notion that since only a noble soul can produce noble art, objects of art should be seen as emblems of the moral health of society as a whole. He agreed, too, with the converse, that methods of production which encourage individual expression can ennoble the worker, and that the spread of such methods can ennoble society. But the specific direction of Morris' own writing comes from his development of the assumption behind the Ruskinian aesthetic, the romantic belief that each man possesses an instinctive imaginative power. The moralization of the creative impulse by Ruskin had drawn the potential clergymen of the Brotherhood to the profession of art which, being sensual, had generally been considered sinful. But by the time Morris began to write about art and society late in his career,[5] he had left the religious ideas of his youth far behind. His main contribution is the secularization of Ruskin. For Morris saw artistic expression not in the Christian terms of Ruskin, as the expression of delight in the world God had made, but in more "modern" terms, as the release of instinctive energies repressed by the rigid patterns of mechanized society: "What is meant by *art* . . . is, I contend, no mere accident to human life, which people can take or leave as they choose, but a positive necessity of life, if we are to live as nature meant us to."[6] The substitution of "as nature meant us to" for "as God meant us to" has far-reaching implications for his social as well as his aesthetic theory.

This notion of true art as the expression of energies stifled by the ordinary conditions of modern life drew confirmation from his own experience. Once he had found his true vocation as a designer-craftsman, this work remained the source of strength at which he would renew himself for his activity in the practical matters of business and politics. He often rose early to get in a few hours at the loom before attending to the problems of the firm or lecturing on socialism. And yet having found in his craft an outlet for his own abundant energies, as well as an escape from a less than happy marriage, he was perhaps too eager in elevating pattern-designing and handwork into the *summum bonum*.

Following the praise of "Savageness" and "Grotesqueness" in "The Nature of Gothic," Morris also takes imperfection as his aesthetic criterion. But he associates this Ruskinian aesthetic value less with religion than with the pervasive nineteenth-century primitivism. Morris takes as the measure of art and the goal of the socialist revolution what he calls "the art of the

people," and finds it not in the religious carving of the
Middle Ages but in its folk art that created secular objects both for decoration and for use.

> A peasant art, I say, and it clung fast to the life of the
> people, and still lived among the cottagers and yeomen
> in many parts of the country while the big houses were
> being built "French and fine": still lived also in many
> a quaint pattern of loom and printing-block, and em-
> broiderer's needle, while over-seas stupid pomp had
> extinguished all nature and freedom, and art was be-
> come, in France especially, the mere expression of that
> successful and exultant rascality, which in the flesh no
> long time afterwards went down into the pit for ever.[7]

In the essay entitled "Art of the People," he celebrates
this primitive work by comparing its expressiveness to
the instinctive release of energy in animals:

> That thing which I understand by real art is the ex-
> pression by man of his pleasure in labour. I do not
> believe he can be happy in his labour without express-
> ing that happiness; and especially is this so when he is
> at work at anything in which he specially excels. A
> most kind gift is this of nature, since all men, nay, it
> seems all things too, must labour; so that not only does
> the dog take pleasure in hunting, and the horse in
> running, and the bird in flying, but so natural does the
> idea seem to us, that we imagine to ourselves that the
> earth and the very elements rejoice in doing their
> appointed work.[8]

But Morris' response to the "art of the people"
surviving in the nineteenth century is curious. In a
manner anticipating the discovery of African art in the
twentieth century, he praises the primitive art of coun-

tries being "civilized" by England and laments the disappearance of native work under the flood of cheap machine-made goods. As usual, this aesthetic judgment of machine work is part of a more general social comparison of the sensual freedom of primitive life with the repressed life of mechanized society:

> The Indian or Javanese craftsman may no longer ply his craft leisurely, working a few hours a day, in producing a maze of strange beauty on a piece of cloth: a steam-engine is set a-going at Manchester, and that victory over Nature and a thousand stubborn difficulties is used for the base work of producing a sort of plaster of china-clay and shoddy, and the Asiatic worker, if he is not starved to death outright, as plentifully happens, is driven himself into a factory to lower the wages of his Manchester brother worker, and nothing of character is left him except, most like, an accumulation of fear and hatred of that to him most unaccountable evil, his English master. The South Sea Islander must leave his canoe-carving, his sweet rest, and his graceful dances, and become the slave of a slave: trousers, shoddy, rum, missionary, and fatal disease—he must swallow all this civilization in the lump, and neither himself nor we can help him now till social order displaces the hideous tyranny of gambling that has ruined him.[9]

And yet although somewhat influenced by the example of Persian carpets, Morris generally took little interest in contemporary folk arts. Although he toured Iceland and absorbed its literary traditions into his poetry, he ignored its native crafts.[10] The force of Victorian medievalism was too strong for him to reach out to other cultures, and he could only seek a primitive art for himself primarily in the work of the Middle Ages. He learned to weave by studying medieval sources and found substitutes for the new aniline dyes in a medieval herbal.

For the destruction of primitive art, Morris did not blame the machine itself, but the division of labor by which the instinctual nature of work is destroyed by its analysis into component parts. In the organic process of work, as in the study of organic life, "we murder to dissect," and the applicability of the Wordsworthian tag indicates that for Morris, as for Ruskin, the source of opposition to mechanized production lay in their sense of the incompatibility between the romantic notions of the plastic arts as intuitive creations and the new, rationalized methods of mechanized work. As a symbol for what he felt was the destructive analysis of the organically unified process of creation, Morris consistently uses the machine:

> Whereas under the eighteenth-century division of labour system, a man was compelled to work for ever at a trifling piece of work in a base mechanical way, which, also, in that base way he understood, under the system of the factory and almost automatic machine under which we now live, he may change his work often enough, may be shifted from machine to machine, and scarcely know that he is producing anything at all: in other words, under the eighteenth-century system he was reduced to a machine; under that of the present day he is the slave to a machine.[11]

To explain Morris' opposition to machine-art by the mechanistic-organic antithesis is to show the terms of the argument rather than its source. For, unlike Ruskin,

Morris was a craftsman before he became a theoretician, and many of his later arguments are drawn from his experience in his own firm. He saw that the vast improvements in machinery spread the division of labor by enabling a small group of designers to furnish the patterns to be repeated endlessly by machines watched over by unskilled workers. His objections to this are often practical, rather than theoretical or moral. Testifying as an expert witness before the Royal Commission on Technical Instruction, he said:

> I think it is a thing to be rather deprecated that there should be a class of mere artists . . . who furnish designs, as it were, ready made, to what you may call the technical designers, the technical designers having next to nothing to do with the drawing, but having what you call the grinding work to do. The designer learns about as much as is necessary for his work from the weaver, in a perfunctory and dull sort of manner, and the result is not so satisfactory as it would be if a different system were adopted.[12]

Here again, Morris' main concern is not eliminating the machine but halting the division of labor. His ideal, in theory if not in practice, is exemplified in the craftsman who through long experience can conceive a design suited to the medium and, in the execution, alter the original plan to suit the unique qualities of the material.

This instinctual, unified creative activity Morris consistently saw, not as the expression of a God-given soul, but simply as a form of sensual pleasure valuable in and of itself. Over and over, in virtually every lecture and essay he told his audience: "The chief duty of the civilized world to-day is to set about making labour happy for all."[13] This continuous chipping was necessary to wear away the pervasive evangelical doctrine that, equating work with duty rather than pleasure, believed the more onerous the task, the more honorable the worker who endures it. The belief in work as duty enabled Carlyle to find nobility in industrial toil and soothed the minds of English factory owners. Only by moving from the idea of work as duty, and even from the Ruskinian idea of creative work as worship, could Morris move to his utopian vision of the machine as the means of releasing repressed sensual energy.

Even in Morris' vision of satisfying work itself, the machine is not excluded. Again, his aim is to liberate the natural impulses of creative work and, as long as machine work can be subordinated to these impulses, it becomes not only tolerable but valuable. He knew that continuous creative effort is impossible; within his own busy routine of composing poetry, running a business, and designing patterns, he found relaxation in the repetitive work of the loom. "Even mechanical labour is pleasant to some people (to me amongst others) if it be not too mechanical,"[14] he said. The two meanings of the word "mechanical" indicate his distinction between the use of the machine and the imposition of its repetitive pattern. In describing "The Factory as It Might Be," he does not eliminate "mechanical labour" but only a pattern of work that is "too mechanical." This essay seeks to answer the question of how society can retain the productive power of the machine without destroying the inherent pleasure of work. His solution here, as in *News from Nowhere*, places pleasure

ahead of production; men satisfy their need for soothing repetitive work by tending the efficient machines
for a few hours and then spend the remainder of the
day in more creative occupations. In this essay, the
balanced social and aesthetic criticism of Morris is at
its best, neither an Arcadian rejection of the machine
in the manner of Ruskin, nor an adulation of its power
in the manner of Carlyle, but a description of how it
may be used to enrich emotional life.

ii

Morris differs from the other writers discussed in
that his social and aesthetic criticism grow from his own
practical experience as businessman and artist. Once his
achievement is separated from pious legend[15] it becomes
clear that the central theme of his career, in his designing as in his writing, is not opposition to the machine
but the desire to find for the machine its proper function. As the firm of Morris and Company grew, it moved
further from its original Ruskinian aim of freeing the
worker. Its goal became primarily the production of
goods of the highest quality, an endeavor in which Morris was quite willing to use the machine.

Morris, Marshall, Faulkner & Co. was established
by a group of young enthusiasts inspired by the Ruskin
they had read in college. Some, like Burne-Jones and
Philip Webb, an architect, were professionals in the
arts; others, like Faulkner and Marshall, a mathemati-
cian and a sanitary engineer respectively, were zealous
amateurs. At first, no one specialized. Each would try
his hand at painting tiles, decorating furniture, or

whatever other work happened to be at hand. But as business increased, the division of labor appeared in what Morris wrote of as its most dangerous form, the distinction between the designer and the executor of the design. In the late 1860's, the firm began receiving large commissions, such as decorating the Green Dining Room at the South Kensington Museum, that could not be completed by part-time amateurs. Morris was forced to take on workmen and set them to the task of carrying out the ideas of the firm's principals. Yet, in these early years, Morris still tried to ignore economic considerations in order to minimize specialization among the workmen. In 1867 George Warrington Taylor, the hard-headed business manager of the company from 1865 to 1870, complained in a letter to Philip Webb: "Baring [a competitor] has a separate staff for each branch of the business—With 12 men being made to do one day one thing one day another—We can only have disorder."[16]

But as the firm prospered, the division between designer and workman grew. In 1875, after unpleasant financial bickering, the amateur members sold their shares, and Morris' pre-eminence was acknowledged in the firm's new title, Morris and Company. In this later phase, the organization came more and more to use outside artistic consultants. Webb and Burne-Jones, both absorbed in their own careers, were associated with the firm solely as part-time designers, and their account books[17] show that they took little or no part in the execution of their work. In Webb's account book there are only a few entries for actual handwork done, and these are all dated before 1866. Yet the firm still tried to minimize specialization, if only among its designers; neither Webb nor Burne-Jones limited himself to creating patterns for a single medium. For example, Webb's account book lists payments for designing stained glass, furniture, drinking glasses, tiles, and paper hangings.

Burne-Jones, too, was primarily a designer working in various media. His main contributions were patterns for the stained-glass windows that were a mainstay of the company's prosperity and figures for Morris tapestries. His account books list virtually no payments for the execution of work. The manner in which his sketches were turned into tapestries illustrates how far Morris and Company had departed from the ideal of the artisan-designer that Morris had proposed as an alternative to mechanized production and also how the firm was willing to use technology as long as it did not detract from the main goal of quality. The painter's sketches were neither full-sized nor colored. According to Aymer Vallance, a close associate of Morris in the firm: "It was necessary for each of these drawings to be enlarged by photography, in squares varying in size and number according to the full dimensions required. These enlarged sections were then fitted together, and the whole, now of the proper size, submitted, together with a small coloured sketch showing the scheme of colouring proposed by the firm, to the designer for his approval or revision." Although the tapestry-weaver was assigned a pattern and color scheme, he was allowed a limited range of originality in execution; for, as Vallance's comments indicate, the firm always held as its ideal the elimination of that unnatural repetitive labor symbolized by the machine. Vallance notes: "Considerable latitude in the choice and arrangement of tints in shading, &c., was, and is, invariably allowed to the executants themselves, who are, in fact, both by nature and training, artists and no mere animated machines."[18] But as Valance admits, when it seemed that the aesthetic quality of the design might be compromised, Morris was quite willing to assign his workers imitative, uncreative tasks. In producing stained-glass windows from Burne-Jones's patterns, "That Mr. Morris felt as keenly as anyone could feel the danger of glass executed by one man from the paper cartoon of another losing its spirit and finer qualities in the process of reproduction is a fact. And accordingly he made a special point of insisting on the literal preservation of every characteristic of the original design with the minutest fidelity possible."[19]

Morris, too, was primarily a designer for his own firm rather than a craftsman. He differed from contemporary designers chiefly in his devotion to mastering the intricate details of process. The laborious experiments by which he rediscovered in medieval sources the arts of dyeing and tapestry-weaving are cases in point. But once the process was mastered, once the formulas were established and the looms set up, he turned the actual execution over to others and confined himself to designing for the new medium. For example, once he had personally decided on the best methods for producing wallpaper, he transferred the entire operation, block-cutting as well as printing, to an outside firm and confined himself to sketching the original patterns on large sheets of paper.

In his business correspondence, Morris is quite clear about his goals. He wrote an associate: "I am sure you understand that we want to get something quite different from the ordinary goods in the market: this is the very heart of our undertaking."[20] According to his Ruskinian theory, happy workers should quite naturally create beautiful objects, but under the daily pressures of business Morris often found it necessary to choose between beautiful objects and happy workers, and in such cases he was more inclined to sacrifice the latter. When the firm occupied cramped quarters in London, he was compelled to have his textile-printing done by the firm of Wardle and Company in Leek. His letters to Thomas Wardle, filled with complaints about poor color and sloppy printing, indicate how Morris cared less for the artistic freedom of the distant operatives than for the appearance of the fabrics. He wrote that the variations introduced by workers nullified "whatever advantage may be derived from my artistic knowledge and taste, *on which the whole of my business depends*: however the subject of these monsters of idiocy is a dismal one and I will say no more than to beg you to impress on them the necessity of following out their instructions to the letter *whatever may be the results*."[21] Eventually, Morris brought textile-printing and dyeing into his enlarged quarters at Merton Abbey so that he could supervise his subordinates more closely.

Merton Abbey exemplifies the Victorian dream of absorbing technology into a pastoral world. The long building rested in unspoiled countryside along the Wandle, whose pure water was used to wash the firm's textiles. Dyed cloth, set out to bleach, speckled the green fields.[22] Within this workshop, Morris allowed certain machines, the hand loom and even a Jacquard loom, a more complicated device in which the textile design is translated into a perforated paper pattern that can guide the machine through endless repetitions. Yet, like Ruskin, he tolerated machinery but hated steam. When thinking of installing his Jacquard, he wrote to Wardle: "As to the loom we should *by all means* want it big enough to weave the widest cloth that can be done well without steampower."[23] In explanation, it must be remembered that the steam engine, even in the last decades of the nineteenth century, was still a clanging, sooty object. To Morris, who shared Ruskin's sensibilities, smoke and noise were not only aesthetically intolerable but also emotionally irreconcilable with the dream of pastoral calm and the vision of a medieval workshop.

Though he banished steam from his own pastoral enclave, he had no hesitations about using steam-powered technology located elsewhere. As always, his criterion was the artistic quality of the product and with a basic sense of functionalism, he saw no objections to using the machine where its exact and repetitive qualities were aesthetically right. His demanding artistic judgments kept the amount of work actually done by machinery small, but in general he followed in practice the principle he emphasized in his lectures: "To refuse altogether to use machine-made work unless where the nature of the thing made compels it, or where the machine does what mere human suffering would otherwise have to do."[24]

He believed that mechanization could best be applied to the production of woven textiles. Assuming, as usual, that work demanding the most self-expression from the artisan has the highest value, he felt that "the noblest of the weaving arts is Tapestry, in which there is nothing mechanical."[25] But for the production of more common fabrics, Morris concluded on the basis of practical experience that the use of the machine was perfectly justified. In ordinary weaving, he notes:

> Its interest is limited by the fact that it is mechanical; since the manner of doing it has with some few exceptions varied little for many hundred years: such trivial alterations as the lifting the warp-threads by means of the Jacquard machine, or throwing the shuttle by steam-power, ought not to make much difference in the art of it, though I cannot say that they have not done so. On the other hand, though mechanical, it produces beautiful things, which an artist cannot disregard.[26]

In his business, Morris made use of modern, steam-powered textile machinery. While in the crowded shop at Queen Square, he had his textile patterns woven by other firms on power-driven looms. He became dissatisfied with outside machine work not because of the process itself, but, as with textile-printing, because he could not keep a close check on the quality of the operation. After moving to more spacious quarters at Merton Abbey, he had most of the work done under his own eye through the mechanical Jacquard process, but still designed some patterns to be done on power looms.

Machinery was barred from the production of printed textiles, but in choosing a hand rather than machine process, Morris, as usual, was guided less by ethical than by artistic considerations. At Merton Abbey specialized workmen stamped the cloth by hand with wooden blocks cut from Morris' own designs, an operation only slightly less repetitive and monotonous than that of their counterparts tending printing machines. Yet, as Peter Floud has shown, Morris' method of hand-printing has definite artistic advantages because it does not limit the width of the pattern to the size of the machine roller and, since with hand-printing each color must dry before the next is applied, this method allows the use of thick, opaque tones.[27]

But, in spite of his emphasis on handwork, Morris never realized his dream of countering mechanized production by restoring a true art of the people. At Merton Abbey, although some men hand-printed textiles while others wove on handlooms, each specialized group was carrying out the ideas of the master-designers, Morris, Webb, and Burne-Jones. This division of labor between artist and worker and the specialization among the workers themselves left the ordinary employee of Morris and Company with an essentially imitative task. Yet, although the firm fell short of Morris' ideal of integrated labor, it did provide many workers with some scope for originality and far more interesting work than the regularized repetition of a mechanized factory. In the midst of the machine age, Morris did succeed in creating and sustaining a group of men whose work was more artistically demanding and probably more satisfying than that of the average factory worker passively watching a machine.

If Morris partially succeeded in restoring the

natural delight in work to his own employees, his equation of true art with self-expression prevented him from creating a modern art of the people. Confident of an inevitable social revolution, he believed that the aim, adopted by the twentieth century, of improving the quality of machine-made goods was only a compromise with a temporary system, and so he made little personal effort to improve mass-produced items. Although he furnished well-known English firms with about twenty patterns for power-woven carpets, he was far more concerned with the problems involved in producing his own company's hand-knotted Hammersmith rugs. Moreover, he disliked reproductions of his work because they not only violated his artistic standards but also threatened his profits. He wrote to Wardle asking him to keep the cost of hand-printing as low as possible: "I must also remind you how much we suffer from imitators. These will be all agog as soon as they hear of our printed cloths being admired, and we must try not to give them the advantage of grossly underselling us . . . I don't think you should look forward to our *ever* using a machine."[28] In an economic system which suddenly had the ability to produce inexpensive machine-made goods, Morris, by refusing to concentrate on aesthetically proper ways of using the machine, inevitably found himself creating luxury products for a wealthy clientele. Whenever he utilized modern machinery, he was able to lower his prices significantly, but handwork predominated and his firm used its own products to decorate the homes of those few people who could afford its services.

Although Morris and Company was engaged in producing art for the rich, its work did set an aesthetic standard for the machine-made goods available to the poor. But Morris' part in moving the taste of his time toward the machine aesthetic of functional simplicity has been greatly exaggerated. He rejected the excessive Victorian love of ornaments which could be produced with such ease by the machine, "the modern, mean, miserable, uncomfortable, and showy, plastered about with wretched sham ornament, trumpery of cast-iron, and brass and polished steel, and what not—offensive to look at, and a nuisance to clean."[29] His motto was *"Have nothing in your houses that you do not know to be useful, or believe to be beautiful,"*[30] and he told his audiences: "I have never been in any rich man's house which would not have looked the better for having a bonfire made outside of it of nine-tenths of all that it held."[31] Yet these often-quoted statements are more an attack on Victorian acquisitiveness than an indictment of the ornamental style. The direction of Morris' own design was not toward simplicity. His genius lay in the ability tastefully to employ intricate pattern and luxuriant ornament. His wallpapers, carpet and textile designs succeed because he can subordinate to an over-all pattern the naturalistic foliage and three-dimensional depth of conventional Victorian design.[32] This acceptance of the Victorian aesthetic of redundance and naturalism sets Morris apart from the designers who were using the machine to create the spare, functional objects that are the true source of modern design.

The most fruitful aesthetic notion that Morris

practiced as well as preached was the Ruskinian ideal of artistic truthfulness. He saw that one reason for the ugliness of Victorian decoration was the use of the machine for such inappropriate tasks as imitating hand-decoration or making one material resemble another. Using Ruskin's dictum that the finished product should show the nature of its manufacture, he advocated in his writing and carried out in his work the principle that machine-made goods, though usually inferior, should unashamedly proclaim their origin: "If you have to design for machine-work, at least let your design show clearly what it is. Make it mechanical with a vengeance, at the same time as simple as possible. Don't try, for instance, to make a printed plate look like a hand-painted one: make it something which no one would try to do if he were painting by hand, if your market drive you into printed plates: I don't see the use of them myself."[33] But Morris, for all his perception of the true nature of mechanized production, could never accept it fully because like Ruskin he saw the finest art as a result of self-expression and the imitation of organic form, and he knew that for this kind of work the machine was unsuited.

Morris' legacy to the machine age was not only the principle of functionalism but the deeper principle, exemplified in both his writing and his practical activity, that beautifying the surroundings of daily life was a concern worthy of the most intense effort. For that purpose he gathered what he considered the finest artistic talent of Victorian England and to that end he used every resource, from a medieval herbal to mechanized weaving, to create objects that matched his high artistic standards.

iii

For Morris, as for Ruskin, the criticism of society is implicit in the idea of art. Each associated art with an instinctive creative impulse and each saw this impulse suppressed and distorted by causes that were extrinsic to art, by a mechanistic psychology that saw men as engines capable of rationalized activity, by a commercial ethos that considered men as machines to be used for the production of material goods. For this constellation of repressive elements, technological and economic, intellectual and ethical, Morris, like Ruskin, used the symbol of the machine.

By the 1870's, when Morris first began to lecture on art and society, the pejorative sense of the machine as symbol had become so generally established that he could use it, virtually without explanation, in his socialist speeches to workingmen. One example can serve for many: "It is not this or that tangible steel and brass machine which we want to get rid of, but the great intangible machine of commercial tyranny, which oppresses the lives of all of us."[34] The machine symbol becomes central to his rhetoric as he draws on its varied meanings to convince his audience that he is not seeking merely the destruction of machinery, nor even purely economic reform, but an entire reorganization of psychic life. For example, he begins a passage in "How We Live and How We Might Live" with a description of the historical fact of mechanization as a cause of "how we live" but as he continues, the word "mechanical" becomes a pejorative adjective describing the quality of emotional life:

> The necessity which forced the profit-grinders to collect their men first into workshops working by the division of labour, and next into great factories worked by machinery, and so gradually to draw them into the great towns and centres of civilization, gave birth to a distinct working-class or proletariat: and this it was which gave them their *mechanical* existence, so to say.[35]

As the essay proceeds, words derived from "machine" continue to function as terms of value, implicitly contrasting the destructive competition between workers with the fellowship of socialism and the regularized work of the factory with a free, instinctive life:

> But note, that they are indeed combined into social groups for the production of wares, but only as yet mechanically; they do not know what they are working at, nor whom they are working for, because they are combining to produce wares of which the profit of a master forms an essential part, instead of goods for their own use: as long as they do this, and compete with each other for leave to do it, they will be, and will feel themselves to be, simply a part of those competing firms I have been speaking of; they will be in fact just a part of the machinery for the production of profit.[36]

The phrase "part of the machinery," then, by evoking the entire organic-mechanistic antithesis, ties the economic critique of industrialism to the more generalized criticism of the psychic unnaturalness of mechanized society.

If the symbol of the machine formed the essential rhetorical link between the Marxist and Ruskinian elements in Morris' social criticism, it had no place in his poetry. His imaginative writing is quite frankly escapist. Personally, its composition provided a diversion from his business and domestic difficulties; he found its moral justification in its providing his readers with a similar escape from the mechanized world. But the escape lay not merely to a world of artificial beauty but to a world in which the passions have been freed, not merely those of joyous sensuality but of sexual jealousy and even of perversion. Thus the seemingly contradictory themes of his poetry, its languid beauty and its hard realism, its chivalry and its brutality are elements within a single consistent theme, the presentation of a life more vital, less repressed than that of mechanized England. The death in the rain by "The Haystack in the Floods" and the perverse activity of the Lord of Utterbol in *Well at the World's End* are, in their demonstration of psychic energy, as much an alternative to effete modern life as is the beauty of the descriptive songs in *The Earthly Paradise*. And the machine can enter such poetry only to define the world for which the poet provides an alternative. Morris introduces his most ambitious poem, *The Earthly Paradise*:

> Forget six counties overhung with smoke,
> Forget the snorting steam and piston stroke,
> Forget the spreading of the hideous town;
> Think rather of the pack-horse on the down,
> And dream of London, small and white and clean.[37]

Only in the later, political poetry describing the oppressiveness of mechanized capitalist society could the figure of the machine appear. In the *Pilgrims of Hope* (1885–86), a long love story set in the time of the Paris Commune, Morris employs machine imagery throughout a section called "Meeting the War-Machine," which describes the capitalist attack on the city:

> For indeed a very machine is the war that now
>   men wage;
> Nor have we hold of its handle, we gulled of our
>   heritage,
> We workmen slaves of machines. Well it ground
>   us small enough
> This machine of the beaten Bourgeois; though
>   oft the work was rough
> That it turned out for its money.[38]

But here, even though the machine as metaphor is again meant to combine the ideas of economic power and psychic destructiveness, the figure does not develop out of the visual image of any specific machine, as it does in, for example, *Hard Times*; in its abstraction it remains the dead metaphor of propaganda.

As the term "war-machine" indicates, in the last decades of the century the literature of the machine began to concentrate less on the mechanization of production and more on the mechanization of warfare. Dickens, always strongly nationalistic, had in the 1860's described with pride the powerful machinery building England's ironclads at the Chatham shipyards. Ruskin, on the other hand, in a speech in 1865 warned the military cadets at Woolwich of the destructive capabilities of military technology.[39] Morris' response to military technology was also fear rather than pride; he continually warns his audience against such "preposterous follies as the invention of anthracine colours and monster cannon."[40] But the full imaginative absorption of the Maxim gun, nitroglycerine, and aerial warfare came only with the next generation; for Wells and Kipling, the symbolic use of technology develops most frequently out of the machine as weapon.

To control the machine, Morris looked to socialism. He was drawn into political questions in the 1870's by taking a public stand against English involvement in the Russo-Turkish War and against the improper restoration of old buildings. As important as the pull of events in leading him to socialism, though, was the internal logic of the Ruskinian aesthetic. For it was but a short step from Ruskin to Marx. Both believed, to quote Morris, that "the art of any epoch must of necessity be the expression of its social life,"[41] but whereas Ruskin spoke of the intangible influence of moral ideals, Marx pointed to the materialistic effects of a capitalistic economy. Since by the 1870's it seemed clear that a Ruskinian moral revolution was less than likely, Morris was drawn to the ideas of economic necessity. His political ideas remained a curious mixture, Marxist in the expectation of revolutionary class warfare, Ruskinian in the emphasis on social reform as a means of improving not productivity but the quality of emotional life. Socialism is defined not in economic terms but in terms of the Carlyle-Ruskin vision of the psychic malaise of industrial life cured through the creation of an organic society. Just as Morris' secularization of the Ruskinian aesthetic provides a transition from the Victorian morality of art to the modern celebration of primitive art, his secularization of the Ruskinian social ideal turns Victorian medievalism into twentieth-century primitivism. Freed of its longing for an unquestioned Christian faith, the antimachine medievalism of Carlyle and Ruskin easily expresses, in *News from Nowhere*, the desire for a richer sensual life.

News from Nowhere is far more than an anti-machine tract. Specifically, it was intended as a direct reply to Edward Bellamy's *Looking Backward* (1887), an immensely popular utopian work describing the material benefits that would flow from the efficient use of machine technology. In Bellamy's Boston of the future, music is piped into every room and rich merchandise delivered speedily to every home by pneumatic tube. Morris includes equally fantastic devices in his own utopia; what he objects to in Bellamy's scheme is not its technology but its basic premise—that the individual can find satisfaction through curbing his emotional life in order to enjoy the comforts created by the machine. In *Looking Backward*, everyone must join the industrial army and work at his assigned task until old age; after reading the book, Morris told his daughters that he "wouldn't care to live in such a Cockney paradise as he [Bellamy] imagines . . . if they brigaded *him* into a regiment of workers he would just lie on his back and kick."[42]

The great vogue of Bellamy's book indicates the popularity of his thesis. To renounce the notion that multiplying machine-made goods can multiply happiness is to continue the radical implications of Ruskin's redefinition of wealth. This opposition between machine-made wealth and satisfaction seemed to Morris, as to other Victorians, a re-enactment of the myth of Midas. Carlyle had summed up the disappointed hopes of the early Victorians in the "Proem" to *Past and Present*, entitled "Midas":

> With unbated bounty the land of England blooms and grows; waving with yellow harvests; thick-studded with workshops, industrial implements, with fifteen millions of workers . . . these men are here; the work they have done, the fruit they have realised is here . . . and behold, some baleful fiat as of Enchantment has gone forth, saying, "Touch it not, ye workers, ye master-workers, ye master-idlers; none of you can touch it, no man of you shall be the better for it; this is enchanted fruit!"[43]

Of a later generation, Morris was spared the process of disenchantment with the machine, but used the same myth to describe not the unequal distribution of machine-made wealth but the disparity between this wealth and emotional well-being: "The world had to learn another lesson; it had to gain power, and not be able to use it; to gain riches, and starve upon them like Midas on his gold . . . in a word, to be so eager to gather the results of the deeds of the life of man that it must forget the life of man itself."[44]

In opposition to the goal of productivity, Morris sets up as his standard of value what he calls "nature." In distinguishing between wealth and "illth," Ruskin, too, associates what is valuable with what is natural, but in his sacramental view closeness to nature implies closeness to God; in Morris' secular vision, closeness to nature implies closeness to self. Beneath the Victorian propriety which Morris the revolutionary never transgressed, *News from Nowhere* describes how men must turn for their fulfillment to the sources of sensual delight within themselves; a resident of the future asks:

> Was not their [the Victorians'] mistake once more bred of the life of slavery that they had been living?—a life which was always looking upon everything, except mankind, animate and inanimate—"nature," as people used to call it—as one thing, and mankind as another. It was natural to people thinking in this way, that they should try to make "nature" their slave, since they thought "nature" was something outside them.[45]

Throughout, the book suggests that the overthrow of capitalism will liberate a range of natural energies beyond those associated only with art. In its secular and psychological frame of reference, *News from Nowhere* provides a transition between the Victorian and the twentieth-century response to the machine by taking the generalized Victorian sense of the emotional repressiveness of mechanized life and restating this theme in explicitly sexual terms.

The conflict between sexuality and mechanization, so familiar in the works of twentieth-century writers, is implicit throughout Victorian literature. *Hard Times* shows Louisa's sexual passions, symbolized by the fires of Coketown, smothered beneath the mechanistic educational scheme and flaring out dangerously in later life. The sexual suggestiveness with which Tennyson in "Locksley Hall" describes the primitive life indicates its attractiveness:

> There the passions cramp'd no longer shall have
>   scope and breathing-space;
> I will take some savage woman, she shall rear my
>   dusky race.
> Iron-jointed, supple-sinew'd, they shall dive, and
>   they shall run,
> Catch the wild goat by the hair, and hurl their
>   lances in the sun.[46]

Of course, Tennyson's hero rejects this vision for "this march of mind, / In the steamship, in the railway, in the thoughts that shake mankind."[47] But Morris' Victorian visitor to the pastoral utopia of the future has no doubts about the value of its sensual delights. The men are muscular, the girls nut-brown, and the narrator, speaking for Morris, can hardly conceal his joy in the pleasures of flirtation and the ease of divorce. Even his metaphor for this ideal life is explicitly sexual: "The spirit of the new days, of our days, was to be delight in the life of the world; intense and overweening love of the very skin and surface of the earth on which man dwells, such as a lover has in the fair flesh of the woman he loves."[48]

In his utopia, as in his essays and his commercial practice, Morris saw no necessary conflict between the machine and the sensually liberated life. Like Carlyle, Dickens, and even Ruskin, he shared the Victorian delight in technological achievement. In his success in organizing the manifold activities of Morris and Company, he exemplifies the commercial energy of the machine age. And his craftsman's admiration of the functional beauty of machinery only exacerbated his rage at its uses; the historian in *News from Nowhere* speaks for Morris in saying:

> There was one class of goods which they [the nine-teenth century] did make thoroughly well, and that was the class of machines which were used for making things. These were usually quite perfect pieces of work-manship, admirably adapted to the end in view. So that it may be fairly said that the great achievement of the nineteenth century was the making of machines which were wonders of invention, skill, and patience, and which were used for the production of measureless quantities of worthless make-shifts.[49]

In his vision of the perfect society, the machine is put to its proper use, not the multiplication of objects, but the liberation of men entirely from the necessity of repressive work. Throughout his writings he insists that improved machinery take over the necessary but tedious physical tasks:

> I want modern science, which I believe to be capable of overcoming all material difficulties, to turn . . . to the invention of machines for performing such labour as is revolting and destructive of self-respect to the men who now have to do it by hand.[50]

And in his utopia, he describes this new machinery with an imaginative grasp of its potential equal to that of Wells or Kipling. Freed from the Victorian doctrine of work, Morris can see the machine as a new Caliban, able to perform all unpleasant labor so that its masters could enjoy a sensual, creative life. The utopians employ, in Morris' vague but confident phrase, "immensely improved machinery" to do "all work which would be irksome to do by hand."[51] The visitor to the future sees barges on the Thames

> laden with hay or other country produce, or carrying bricks, lime, timber, and the like, and these were going on their way without any means of propulsion visible to me—just a man at the tiller, with often a friend or two laughing and talking with him.

And he is told: "That is one of our force-barges; it is quite as easy to work vehicles by force by water as by land."[52] Above all, the machinery of the future is aesthetically pleasing. The force barge is a vision of the age of clean power; there is no soot to mar the natural world.

In this utopia, the machine can be both beautiful and useful because it is placed in a society where values have been radically altered, where the end of social life is not production but what Herbert Marcuse in *Eros and Civilization* calls "play," "the play of life itself, beyond want and external compulsion—the manifestation of an existence without fear and anxiety."[53] The utopians say: "This is not an age of inventions. The last epoch did all that for us, and we are now content to use such of its inventions as we find handy, and leaving those alone which we don't want."[54] It is in this vision, in which improved machinery takes over all repressive work in order to free a full range of natural energies, from artistic expression to sexuality, that the Victorian writing on the machine becomes most relevant to the twentieth century.

5 Evolution and the Machine: *Samuel Butler*

Throughout the first half of the nineteenth century, the literary use of the machine metaphor depended for its effect on an implicit contrast to a value-laden complex of organic metaphors derived from a vitalistic biological theory. But by the middle decades of the century, with the success of the Darwinian theory and with advances in scientific physiology, it seemed to biologists that the modern machine, self-powered, often self-regulating, moving predictably by the complex interaction of springs and levers, provided an ideal theoretical model for organic life itself. In 1874 Thomas Henry Huxley, the acknowledged spokesman for science in England, in an essay entitled "On the Hypothesis that Animals are Automata, and Its History," could declare the principle of mechanism as the central hypothesis of modern biology:

> In the seventeenth century, the idea that the physical processes of life are capable of being explained in the same way as other physical phenomena, and, therefore,

that the living body is a mechanism, was proved to be true for certain classes of vital actions; and, having thus taken firm root in irrefragable fact, this conception has not only successfully repelled every assault . . . but has steadily grown in force and extent of application, until it is now the expressed or implied fundamental proposition of the whole doctrine of scientific Physiology.[1]

With the biologists' assertion that men can best be explained as extraordinarily complex machines, the pervasive nineteenth-century problem of philosphical mechanism, with all its deterministic implications, seemed to many Victorians a question best settled by scientific proof. The comparison of man to a machine was no longer a literary figure, but a scientific hypothesis; when Huxley writes on animals as automata, he verifies his hypothesis with experimental data. He concentrates on the question of consciousness; for consciousness, with its qualities of foresight and volition, had throughout the century been the defining characteristic of organic life. Cutting at the central vitalistic position, he asserts that consciousness, the sense of a free and powerful self that to Carlyle had been proof against the encompassing determinism of the world as machine, cannot be considered a cause of biological activity, but only a by-product. As proof, he speaks of experiments in which, with higher centers of the brain removed, frogs could still catch flies and men could still converse. For Huxley, these examples seemed to prove "that in men, as in brutes, there is no proof that any state of consciousness is the cause of change in the motion of the matter of the organism."[2] Convinced of the usefulness of the mechanistic hypothesis, ready to accept the findings of science no matter how disturbing, Huxley is able to use the now familiar figure of the steam engine dispassionately, as a useful scientific premise holding no pejorative connotations: "The consciousness of brutes would appear to be related to the mechanism of their body simply as a collateral product of its working, and to be as completely without any power of modifying that working as the steam-whistle which accompanies the work of a locomotive engine is without influence upon its machinery."[3] Always ready to carry the results of the laboratory to their furthest philosophical implications, Huxley fits the microcosm into the macrocosm, the notion of man as predictable machine into the larger vision of the natural world as predictable machine. This philosophical determinism seemed to many Victorian writers so terrifying that it could not possibly be true; but for Huxley it not only becomes the hypothesis on which scientific speculation must proceed, but also defines the stark world in which man must create his own ethical order: "We are conscious automata, endowed with free will in the only intelligible sense of that much-abused term —inasmuch as in many respects we are able to do as we like—but none the less parts of the great series of causes and effects which, in unbroken continuity, composes that which is, and has been, and shall be—the sum of existence."[4]

But if Huxley found the vision of a mechanistic universe morally bracing, many of his contemporaries found

it significantly less so.* If Huxley could, with equa-
nimity, compare man to a steam engine, other Victorians
were profoundly disturbed by the apparent scientific
sanction given to philosophical mechanism. In 1883
Samuel Butler wrote to his sister: "It is not the bishops
and archbishops I am afraid of. Men like Huxley and
Tyndall are my natural enemies."[5] And in another
letter, three years later, he explains that his own evolutionary treatise, *Luck or Cunning?*, is meant to be "po-
lemical" only in regard to "Mr. Darwin, Professor Huxley, Mr. Romanes and others." The book, he says, "is
directed against the present mindless, mechanical, materialistic view of nature," and "its very essence is to
insist on the omnipresence of a mind and intelligence
throughout the universe to which no name can be so
fittingly applied as God."[6]

But Butler had not always objected so strongly to
Darwinian theories. In his youthful essays on evolution
and the machine, as well as in the first (1872) version of
Erewhon, Butler approaches mechanistic biology with
nearly perfect intellectual ambivalence, with an ironic
detachment that seeks only to play with the paradoxes of
philosophical mechanism rather than resolve them. Only
after *Erewhon* did Butler change from satirist to scientist
as he sought to develop a vitalistic theory that could
supplant the mechanistic system of Darwin.

* This brief discussion cannot do justice to the subtlety of
Huxley's mind. There is much of the mystic in the scientist
who considered all hypotheses, including the mechanistic, not as
true descriptions of the natural world, but as useful models for
describing a reality that is essentially unknowable.

In *Unconscious Memory* (1880), Butler describes his intellectual conversion from mechanistic to vitalistic evolution:

> In 1870 and 1871, when I was writing *Erewhon,* I thought the best way of looking at machines was to see them as limbs which we had made and carried about with us or left at home at pleasure. I was not, however, satisfied, and should have gone on with the subject at once if I had not been anxious to write *The Fair Haven.*
>
> As soon as I had finished this, I returned to the old subject . . . and proposed to myself to see not only machines as limbs, but also limbs as machines. I felt immediately that I was upon firmer ground . . . What would follow, then, if we regarded our limbs and organs as things that we had ourselves manufactured for our convenience?[7]

Although this statement imposes the easy order of hindsight, reducing a process that starts with his earliest writings to a single moment of insight, it does make explicit his realization that only be reinterpreting the comparison of organic life to the machine, the analogy on which nineteenth-century biology depends, could he break away from the deterministic implications of Darwinism.

This conversion to vitalism is, then, a philosophical reinterpretation accomplished through an imaginative shift of metaphor. For Butler the theorist, limbs are still machines, not machines in the common Victorian metaphorical sense used by Huxley—devices acting with the predictability of inanimate matter—but machines in the sense suggested in such early essays as "Lucubratio Ebria" and again in *Erewhon,* machines as the material manifestations of man's conscious or unconscious desire to develop. Such a machine is the organ (the biological pun is striking) Ernest builds in *The Way of All Flesh* as an extension of himself, half-consciously created to express his instinctive musical ability.

In Butler's transformation of the machine metaphor, as in most Victorian use of the machine figure, the responses to philosophical mechanism and to mechanization are closely related. It has been persuasively argued that the essential originality of Darwin lies in his applying to the problem of organic evolution the economic metaphors of social atomism and Malthusian struggle already commonplace in the nineteenth-century attitudes to industrialization.[8] Butler's development of his vitalistic theory, of his belief that organisms create limbs out of an unconscious desire to improve themselves, is an essentially similar intellectual act; for he takes as the central explanatory principle of his evolutionary theory the pervasive Victorian economic justification of machines as devices created by the spirit of man to extend the range of his strength and speed.

The nature of Butler's evolutionary vitalism having been studied in great detail by recent critics,[9] its general outlines need only be considered here. Just as Darwin supplies the few simple principles which explain evolution in terms of uniform natural law, so Butler attempts to become the Darwin of vitalism by setting forth the few "scientific" principles that would reconcile the facts of evolution with vitalistic assumptions. Butler sees evolution as occurring not through the predictable, impersonal operation of regular laws, but through the spontaneous, volitional activity of a life force. Evolutionary change originates in the conscious desire of organisms to reshape their bodies. But over geologic time, the original conscious impulse, like the original act of will that begins an ordinary habit, falls below the level of consciousness. This originally conscious, now unconscious impulse passed on through heredity, Butler calls unconscious memory. The primordial chicken embryo, for example, might have consciously surveyed the possibilities and chosen to develop into a chicken, but all future embryos became chickens through the inherited unconscious memory of this primordial choice. Furthermore, except for having chosen to become a chicken, this volitional energy, according to Butler, does not differ essentially from that of any other living creature. In explaining all evolutionary change by the operation of a single, unified, nonmaterial force, Butler's scientific writings inevitably moved him back to the transcendental terms in which mechanistic science had been opposed throughout the century.

The complexities of Butler's vitalistic theory, its development through his scientific writing, his paranoic quarrels with the Darwinians, are all beyond the scope of this discussion. Of more relevance is his virtually unique imaginative use of the machine as a figure for vitalistic process. If the Huxleyan biologist uses the steam engine as the conceptual model for the predictable activity of a single organism, in his scientific writing Butler consistently refutes mechanistic biology indirectly by making the same analogy serve as model for volitional, creative evolution. The development of the steam en-

gine becomes a proof by analogy that small, consciously
made improvements can, unconsciously, lead to the creation of a new species: "Many, again, of the steps leading
to the present development have been due to action
which had but little heed of the steam engine, being
the invention of attendants whose desire was to save
themselves the trouble of turning this or that cock, and
who were indifferent to any other end than their own
immediate convenience. No step in fact along the whole
route was ever taken with much perception of what
would be the next step."[10] Technological invention is
consistently made the model for the essential paradox
of his theory, conscious design unaware of itself:

> It was as though those who had insisted on the deriva-
> tion of all forms of the steam-engine from the common
> kettle, and who saw that this stands in much the same
> relations to the engines, we will say, of the *Great
> Eastern* steamship as the amoeba to man, were to de-
> clare that the *Great Eastern* engines were not designed
> at all, on the ground that no one in the early kettle
> days had foreseen so great a future development, and
> were unable to understand that a piecemeal *solvitur
> ambulando* design is more omnipresent, all-seeing, and
> all-searching, and hence more truly in the strictest
> sense design, than any speculative leap of fancy.[11]

Even the commonplace Victorian picture of man as
automaton in the mechanized factory is transformed
into an example of the creative unconscious:

> Nor do we find that an engine made after any old and
> well-known pattern is now made with much more
> consciousness of design than we can suppose a bird's
> nest to be built with . . . It is only when circumstances

require any modification in the article to be manufactured that thought and design will come into play
again; but I take it few will deny that if circumstances
compel a bird either to give up a nest three-parts built
altogether, or to make some trifling deviation from its
ordinary practice, it will in nine cases out of ten make
such deviation as shall show that it had thought the
matter over.[12]

i

Butler first began to explore the parallels between
organic life and machinery in a youthful series of essays,
"Darwin among the Machines" (1863), "Lucubratio
Ebria" (1865), and "The Mechanical Creation" (1865).
These early essays on the machine, read now primarily
as sources of *Erewhon* and of Butler's later vitalistic
thought, have a further, literary importance—their creation of a new literary form in which to treat not only the
problem of the machine, but more general social concerns as well. Earlier Victorian writers occupied with
the effects of mechanization had to stay within a generally "realistic" mode, describing the effects of the
mechanized environment on recognizable, contemporary
characters. It is curious, however, how often, even for the
early Victorians, antimachine literature breaks out of
this realistic frame, either into imaginary worlds of the
past or into the surreal world of *Hard Times*. But evolution, which brought a sense of how changes in the environment could create radical physical changes in
organic life itself, and geology, which brought a vastly
expanded time scale, made possible a new form of literature in which changes brought by mechanization could

be visualized by projecting them into the future in extreme, physical form. From the 1860's and 1870's the evolutionary fantasy, rather than the realistic industrial novel, becomes the main vehicle of antimachine criticism. Butler himself never developed this genre fully, although his evolutionary description of mechanization constantly moves him toward social criticism. He says, for example, in "The Mechanical Creation" that machines "will breed, and beyond a doubt, varieties and sub-varieties of the human race will be developed with a special view to the requirements of certain classes of machinery; we can see the germs of this already in the different aspects of men who attend on different classes of machinery."[13] In this suggestion of the evolutionary effects of the division of labor, there is implicit the brutalized Morlocks of Wells's *Time Machine*, the effete citizenry of Kipling's "As Easy as A.B.C." and the chemical wombs of Aldous Huxley's *Brave New World*.

But in his early essays and in the first version of *Erewhon*, Butler uses the evolutionary metaphor less as a vehicle for social criticism than as an intellectual conceit which enables him playfully to exhibit the paradoxes implicit in philosophical mechanism and industrial mechanization. In "Darwin among the Machines," Butler links the commonplace literary notion of the machine as dominating English life with the equally common post-Darwinian fear that a new species would evolve to supersede man. The seriousness with which the Victorians contemplated their own evolutionary decline can be seen in the popularity of Bulwer Lytton's *The Coming Race* (1871) which describes a superior race living underground, biding their time by working, significantly, at their giant machinery.* But Butler's treatment of the same theme has none of Bulwer Lytton's seriousness. Butler introduces the analogy between the origin of species and the origin of machines, an analogy that will later become central to his proof of vitalism, in a thoroughly whimsical tone. Both animals and watches grow smaller and more complex as they develop; vestigial organs linger in animals and tobacco pipes; machines and organisms can both be classified by genera, species, and varieties. He also plays with the Victorian linguistic habit of anthropomorphizing machinery: "If they want 'feeding' (by use of which very word we betray our recognition of them as living organisms) they will be attended by patient slaves whose business and interest it will be to see that they shall want for nothing."[14] And yet, although these comparisons are obviously not made with the serious descriptive and philosophical intent of a Huxley, here, as throughout Butler's early writing, the wit is pointing to, if not resolving, a major philosophical issue. By showing the similar in the dissimilar, the mechanical in the organic, and the organic in the mechanical, Butler is illustrating the paradox that man demonstrates the predictable activity of machines and yet still feels that he possesses free will. If this dilemma is resolved in his later scientific writing by the itself paradoxical idea of unconscious

---

* In his 1872 Preface to *Erewhon* Butler takes great pains to disprove the allegation that *Erewhon* capitalized on the success of *The Coming Race* by showing, quite correctly, that he had held the ideas for the "Book of the Machines" far earlier.

memory, in the early work the literary form suggests only the paradox itself.

The same use of unresolved antitheses structures the social criticism of the essay. The strictures against the machine are the commonplace Victorian assertions that the worker is enslaved to the machine, assertions formerly expressed through the metaphors of oriental despots or angry gods, now put in the new evolutionary metaphor of the coming race: "Day by day, however, the machines are gaining ground upon us; day by day we are becoming more subservient to them; more men are daily bound down as slaves to tend them, more men are daily devoting the energies of their whole lives to the development of mechanical life."[15] But this antimachine position is undercut here, as it will be later and more elaborately in *Erewhon*, by the extreme, often absurd character of the implied author, who becomes almost a caricature of antimachine primitivists such as Ruskin: "Our opinion is that war to the death should be instantly proclaimed against them. Every machine of every sort should be destroyed by the well-wisher of his species. Let there be no exceptions made, no quarter shown; let us at once go back to the primeval condition of the race."[16] Here again the wit points to another paradox of Victorian thought, the paradox of mechanization itself, that men are both enslaved and benefited by the machine. "The fact is that our interests are inseparable from theirs [the machines'], and theirs from ours. Each race is dependent upon the other for innumerable benefits."[17]

The paradoxes of biological mechanism and industrial mechanization ostensibly are set, as the title suggests, within the intellectual framework of Darwinian evolution. He speaks, for example, of "how subservience to the use of man has played that part among machines which natural selection has performed in the animal and vegetable kingdoms."[18] And yet his application of Darwin to the evolution of technology indicates that from the very beginning Butler was never completely in agreement with the mechanistic element of Darwinism, the assumption that evolution is self-regulating under the determining influence of fixed natural laws. Although describing technological progress in Darwinian terms, his figures emphasize what would become the central metaphorical point of his later evolutionary writings, the effect of an unconscious shaping power in developing the machine:

> What sort of creature [is] man's next successor in the supremacy of the earth . . . likely to be. We have often heard this debated; but it appears to us that we are ourselves creating our own successors; we are daily adding to the beauty and delicacy of their physical organization; we are daily giving them greater power and supplying by all sorts of ingenious contrivances that self-regulating, self-acting power which will be to them what intellect has been to the human race.[19]

Committed neither to a mechanistic Darwinism nor to the antimachine literary position, Butler was quite able, indeed anxious, to argue the opposite side. Looking back in later life to these articles, he commented with insouciant pride that after developing in "Darwin among the Machines" the notion that machinery would

supersede man, "I soon felt that though there was plenty
of amusement to be got out of this line, it was one that
I should have to leave sooner or later; I therefore left it
at once for the view that machines were limbs which
we had made, and carried outside our bodies instead
of incorporating them with ourselves."[20] This notion
of machines as limbs is developed with equal wit in his
second essay on machinery, "Lucubratio Ebria," written
after his return to England and sent back to the Christ-
church newspaper where it was published in July 1865.
Here again Butler ostensibly keeps the comparison of
biological and technological evolution within the Darwinian framework, even making explicit the mechanistic
doctrine that organic change is determined by predictable, impersonal laws, "by chances and changes over
which the creature modified had no control whatever,
and concerning whose aim it was alike unconscious and
indifferent."[21] But here, even more than in the first essay, the machine metaphor keeps breaking out of the
Darwinian frame to become a figure for purposeful,
vitalistic evolution. Having developed conscious volition, man, according to Butler, is no longer acted upon
by external laws but creates his own environment
through the purposive development of new machines:
"When human intelligence stole like a late spring upon
the mimicry of our semi-simious ancestry, the creature
learnt how he could of his own forethought add extra-
corporaneous limbs to the members of his own body,
and become not only a vertebrate mammal, but a vertebrate machinate mammal into the bargain."[22]

Associating technological progress with biological

evolution led not only to new metaphors but to new insights. With the increased time scale provided by Darwin and the geologists, men could see that technological change had become the strongest single influence on the development of the human species. "Were it not for this constant change in our physical powers, which our mechanical limbs have brought about, man would have long since apparently attained his limit of possibility; he would be a creature of as much fixity as the ants and bees; he would still have advanced, but no faster than other animals advance."[23] Beneath the whimsy, there is Butler's perception that technology rather than biology is the true measure of human potential: "By the institutions and state of science under which a man is born it is determined whether he shall have the limbs of an Australian savage or those of a nineteenth-century Englishman."[24] Furthermore, the evolutionary metaphors give an almost scientific sanction to the common nineteenth-century pro-machine argument that the machine has expanded the range of human possibility: "It is a mistake, then, to take the view adopted by a previous correspondent of this paper, to consider the machines as identities, to animalize them and to anticipate their final triumph over mankind. They are to be regarded as the mode of development by which human organism is most especially advancing, and every fresh invention is to be considered as an additional member of the resources of the human body."[25]

Butler hoped to continue this wit-combat between his own divided opinions indefinitely, but only one more essay on evolution and the machine, "The Mechanical Creation," reached print. This essay differs little in substance from "Darwin among the Machines" except in its toning down of the antimachine sentiments implied by the figure of machinery as the coming race. Although he points to the problem broached in his first essay, that the quality of life has declined as technology has advanced, his descriptions of mechanization have lost the harshness of the earlier conventional images of slavery. The exaggerated tone even suggests that some passages might be refuting the antimachine critics by setting their strictures against plain bourgeois common sense: "It is true that here and there some ardent soul may 'look upon himself and curse his fate' that he was not born a steam engine, but the insensate mass will readily acquiesce in any arrangement which gives them cheaper comforts without yielding to unreasonable jealousy, merely because the mechanical destinies are more glorious than their own."[26] But, as if recognizing the ambiguity of the essay, he ends with the promise of continuing the debate: "We have proceeded on the assumption that mechanical life is to be distinct from animal, but in a future article we propose to consider if from a different view, and to regard machinery as a component part of the human organism."[27] The article was never written, but the paradoxical positions on biological mechanism and industrial mechanization were taken up with increased wit and equal ambiguity in the first version of *Erewhon*; they were not finally resolved until, having developed his own vitalistic theory, Butler revised *Erewhon* one year before his death.

ii

In the preface to *Erewhon* in 1872, Butler warns his readers that the "Book of the Machines" has been incorrectly read as a refutation of Darwin and suggests that his real satirical target is the "specious misuse of analogy"[28] in another book, probably Joseph Butler's popular religious work, *The Analogy of Religion*. As usual, the statement is itself ambiguous, but it provides an important indication as to the meaning of the "Book of the Machines" in mentioning the "specious misuse of analogy" as the external object of ridicule. If it is an exceedingly indirect attack on the use of analogy in religion, it is more explicitly concerned with the use of the machine analogy in describing organic life. But the satire of the 1872 version of *Erewhon* is unresolved on the question of biological mechanism—only in the last year of his life did he revise the work to make it a defense of vitalism. Similarly, the first version is equally ambivalent in its attitude toward industrial mechanization, but in revising the work for the final version of 1901, Butler added material which turns the work into a satire of Victorian antimachine criticism.

In *Life and Habit* (1877), his first scientific treatise on biological vitalism, he says that once the biologist accepts the machine as a conceptual model for organic life, once he assumes that any animal, even man, is "such and such a machine, of which if you touch such

and such a spring, you will get a corresponding action
. . . he will find, so far as I can see, no escape from a
position very similar to the one which I put into the
mouth of the first of the two professors who dealt with
the question of machinery in my earlier work, *Erewhon*."[29]

The account of the first professor, which makes up
the bulk of the "Book of the Machines," can indeed be
read as a satire in which the external object of ridicule
is biological mechanism, and the method a *reductio ad
absurdum* refutation of the machine analogy. The first
professor, a scientist at the Colleges of Unreason, traces
out the philosophical implications of biological mechanism with a logical rigor worthy of Thomas Henry
Huxley. But without any authorial comment, the reader
can only evaluate the professor's account by shifts in
diction. The professor often begins with restrained
scientific language that appears straight out of Huxley
but moves to rephrasings that are palpably absurd. For
example:

> If it be urged that the action of the potato is chemi-
> cal and mechanical only, and that it is due to the
> chemical and mechanical effects of light and heat, the
> answer would seem to lie in an inquiry whether every
> sensation is not chemical and mechanical in its opera-
> tion? . . . Whether strictly speaking we should not ask
> what kind of levers a man is made of rather than what
> is his temperament?[30]

The final chapter of the "Book of the Machines"
continues to explore the machine analogy but moves
from biological theory to the more general implication

of psychological determinism. Here again Butler tests the mechanistic hypothesis by having the first professor carry it to its logical extreme; here again the testing turns into a refutation of mechanism by showing the absurdity of the deterministic implications. The professor answers the objection that the machine cannot displace man because it lacks volition by using the machine analogy to show that man himself has as little, or as much, volition as a complex modern machine. Butler's philosophical point here, as in the early essays, is that the mechanistic hypothesis necessarily implies a complete philosophical determinism. Again the rhetorical signals for the satire of the first professor and his theory are provided by the shifts of tone, from the scientific statement of the premise, "a man is the resultant and exponent of all the forces that have been brought to bear upon him, whether before his birth or afterwards . . . As he is by nature, and as he has been acted on, and is now acted on from without, so will he do, as certainly and regularly as though he were a machine,"[31] to the whimsical description of the logical conclusion:

> At first sight it would indeed appear that a vapour-engine cannot help going when set upon a line of rails with the steam up and machinery in full play; whereas the man whose business it is to drive it can help doing so at any moment that he pleases . . . The driver is obedient to his masters, because he gets food and warmth from them, and if these are withheld or given in insufficient quantities he will cease to drive; in like manner the engine will cease to work if it is insufficiently fed.[32]

It would be tempting in the light of Butler's later conversion to vitalism to read the "Book of the Machines" in its original context as Butler himself did in his later career, as a spoof of the mechanistic hypothesis. But it is clear that the work as it stands in the 1872 edition is totally ambivalent; if Butler was dissatisfied with the implications of a mechanistic Darwinism, he was equally unsure about the vitalistic alternative. There are no rhetorical signs to indicate that the assertions of biological vitalism are to be taken with any more seriousness than those of biological mechanism. For example, after taking the mechanistic hypothesis to the seemingly untenable conclusion that chemistry could predict temperament from a single hair, he immediately mentions, but only in passing, the central principle of his later vitalistic theory. He says in serious scientific prose that "a great deal of action that has been called purely mechanical and unconscious must be admitted to contain more elements of consciousness than has been allowed hitherto."[33] And yet the examples that follow from this premise are given with the same whimsical tone that is used to show the absurdity in the implications of mechanism: "Even a potato in a dark cellar has a certain low cunning about him which serves him in excellent stead . . . What deliberation he may exercise in the matter of his roots when he is planted in the earth is a thing unknown to us, but we can imagine him saying, 'I will have a tuber here and a tuber there, and I will suck whatsoever advantage I can from all my surroundings.' "[34]

And yet, it is this very ambivalence, this lack of

rhetorical certainty, that makes the "Book of the Machines" such an engaging work. For its only statement is a paradox—man's actions are as predictable as those of a machine, and yet to compare man to a machine, to equate the locomotive with its engineer, is palpably absurd. The attractiveness of the work lies in Butler's skill in using modern technology to express this paradox. Or, to generalize, the delight lies in his ability to play with the modern machine as philosophical metaphor for the central paradox of Western philosophy, the conflict between the deterministic implications of science and the inward apprehension of volitional freedom.

The appeal of the "Book of the Machines" to the modern reader is also in Butler's uncanny ability inadvertently to describe the twentieth century. The Erewhonian "straighteners," for example, meant as a satire of the Anglican clergy, appear as perfect types of the modern psychoanalyst. So, too, with Butler's conscious machines. The vision of two vapor engines sitting outside their shed and watching their offspring frolic is not meant in its context as a prediction of technological development, but as part of his questioning of the mechanistic hypothesis. In an ironic sense that Butler might himself appreciate, the public fears of the twentieth century have caught up with his satire. For the logic of his satire depends on the implicit agreement of the reader that any theory that can show a machine to have the same degree of intellect and consciousness as man must be untrue. But if the nineteenth century feared that the machine would replace man first as laborer, then as artisan, the twentieth fears that it will replace man as thinker. In our time, the public debate over the man-machine analogy concentrates less on the question of physiology, which has been resolved in favor of the mechanists, than on the question of whether thought, and even consciousness, is uniquely human. And so, the "Book of the Machines" can be read in two ways, as an engaging account of the twentieth-century fears of the machine as thinker and, in its historical context, as a spoof of philosophical mechanism.

The "Book of the Machines" considers industrial mechanization with the same ambivalence shown in the treatment of philosophical mechanism. Butler rehearses the argument of "Darwin among the Machines," that the machine will supersede and enslave mankind, and, with increased skill in using evolutionary metaphors, extrapolates the effects of mechanization into a future where men have become "affectionate, machine-tickling aphids."[35] But the opposing, pro-machine viewpoint is also given with no rhetorical signals enabling the reader to choose. In the final chapter, a second professor is quoted as having answered the Erewhonian attack on machinery. He suggests the notion introduced in "Lucubratio Ebria" and turned into evolutionary theory in the scientific works, the idea that men extend their ability by creating new and more efficient limbs through technological progress. "Its author said that machines were to be regarded as a part of man's own physical nature, being really nothing but extracorporeal limbs. Man, he said, was a machinate mammal."[36] As in "Lucubratio Ebria" and the scientific writing, this idea is associated with a more purposive, less mechanistic form of evolution:

> Machines are to be regarded as the mode of development by which human organism is now especially advancing, every past invention being an addition to the resources of the human body. Even community of limbs is thus rendered possible to those who have so much community of soul as to own money enough to pay a railway fare; for a train is only a seven-leagued foot that five hundred may own at once.[37]

If, then, the "Book of the Machines" suggests contradictory views about mechanization as it does about biological mechanism, so too it uses the *reductio* technique to test the criticism of the machine. Butler takes the premise of so much nineteenth-century writing, that the machine is enslaving man, and through the narrative carries it to its logical conclusion, that all machinery must be destroyed. The critical question, then, is whether this method is used here to criticize industrial mechanization or, in a manner similar to that of the philosophical sections, to refute Victorian antimachine critics. I would suggest that the "Book of the Machines" as first written is as ambivalent in its treatment of technological progress as it is in its exploration of biological mechanism. But even the most cursory consideration of Butler's character indicates that he would have increasingly less sympathy with the critics of technological progress. Like Dickens, he was too solid a member of the middle class ever to consider restraining the profit motive as a means of restraining the machine. He considered it his duty to remain, if not rich, at least extremely comfortable, and if prosperity depends on technological progress, so be it. When he returned from New Zealand he invested his capital in companies that manufactured machinery and that used machinery in production. Just as in later life he looked back to see the "Book of the Machines" as a satire on mechanistic biology, so, too, he saw the same ambivalent piece as a satire of antimachine literature. And he added the chapters on "The Views of an Erewhonian Prophet Concerning the Rights of Animals" and "The Views of an Erewhonian Philosopher Concerning the Rights of Vegetables" in the final version not only to establish his vitalistic theory as the norm against which the philosophical discussion is to be judged but also to set up the common bourgeois virtues of comfort and prosperity as the norm against which antimachine arguments are to be compared.

The chapter on the "Views of an Erewhonian Prophet Concerning the Rights of Animals" opens with an unusually direct evaluation of the Erewhonians by the narrator.

> It will be seen from the foregoing chapters that the Erewhonians are a meek and long-suffering people, easily led by the nose, and quick to offer up common sense at the shrine of logic, when a philosopher arises among them, who carries them away through his reputation for especial learning, or by convincing them that their existing institutions are not based on the strictest principles of morality.[38]

The Erewhonians are, of course, the English, and the "philosopher" bears a strong resemblance to Ruskin.

Here, as throughout these added chapters, the destruction of the machines is judged against the norm of what Butler calls "common sense," by which he means an instinctive mode of judgment, rather than purely rationalistic argument. The very form of the work is an attack on reason, showing that just as sophistic logic can lead men, as the narrator says, "to cut their throats in the matter of machinery,"[39] so, too, rationality combined with an overdeveloped moral sense can lead them to give up even the natural process of eating. The added chapters, then, satirize antimachine criticism by showing that an argument which asks men to suppress their natural instinct for pleasure for the sake of an abstract ideal can, when taken to a logical extreme, persuade men to starve themselves to death, again for the sake of moral principle. The suggestion that the philosopher is arguing for the rights of vegetables as an indirect means of attacking prohibitions on meat accurately applies to Butler's own indirect method in arguing for vegetarianism as a means of satirizing the opponents of technological progress: "Many think that this philosopher did not believe his own teaching, and, being in secret a great meat-eater, had no other end in view than reducing the prohibition against eating animal food to an absurdity, greater even than an Erewhonian Puritan would be able to stand."[40]

And yet, even with the additional material, the work as a whole remains ambivalent because it is conceived within the conventions of nineteenth-century antimachine literature. With its fruitful land, its clear skies, its healthy people, the land over the range is the pastoral utopia of the machine age. In typical Victorian fashion, its primitivism is even expressed in terms of the medieval ideal: "They were about as far advanced as Europeans of the twelfth or thirteenth century; certainly not more so."[41] For Butler writing in 1872, as for Morris writing almost twenty years later, the medieval pastoral utopia becomes the metaphor for their belief that physical grace and sensual fulfillment could exist only outside the mechanized world. And so, in its treatment of mechanization, *Erewhon,* for all its wit, dramatizes only the Victorian ambivalence to the machine. It is in part an evocation of the "natural" life that could be regenerated in a world freed from the pattern of the machine, and in part a satire of the dreamy unreality of those writers who envisioned such a utopia.

In using the hypothesis of a conscious locomotive to test biological mechanism, as later in using the development of the steam engine to illustrate creative evolution, Butler is following a typical nineteenth-century rhetorical pattern, exemplified earlier in the century by Carlyle, of using modern technology as a figure for philosophical mechanism. But for all Butler's philosophical wit, his literary use of the machine is neither as rich nor as effective as that of Carlyle, Dickens, or Ruskin. When Carlyle rejects the idea of the universe as a "huge, dead, immeasurable Steam-engine," the machine becomes a complex symbol relating his philosophical rejection of an indifferent universe to his moral outrage at the application of this same mechanistic thought to an industrial society. But

Butler never linked his intellectual objection to mechanistic thought with social or moral criticism. In *Erewhon*, the "Book of the Machines" is a separate text set off from the main narrative; Butler in no way dramatizes the relation between the absence of machinery and the quality of Erewhonian life. Nor, in *Erewhon Revisited*, is the reintroduction of machinery linked to the social and religious transformations the narrator describes. In discussing mechanization, an Erewhonian refers to "the consequences that are already beginning to appear, and which, if I mistake not, will assume far more serious proportions in the future,"[42] but these consequences are nowhere elaborated. This consistent separation in his works between the discussion of intellectual mechanism and industrial mechanization, this failure to turn the machine from an intellectual analogy into a complex symbol indicates Butler's own persistent refusal to recognize the social and psychological implications of the mechanistic philosophy he so intensely distrusted.

The Machine
and the Future:
H. G. Wells

6

From *Past and Present* to *News from Nowhere* the literary response to the machine is expressed through the convention of contrasts, the mechanized present set against an idealized past. But for H. G. Wells, a boy raised in the shabby gentility of lower-middle-class life and rescued from a life sentence as a draper by his scholarship to the South Kensington College of Science, there was little love for his own or his country's past. Science had provided a glorious future for Wells; it might do the same for mankind.

When he finally turned from teaching to the more lucrative career of writing, Wells sought to convey the excitement of scientific speculation that he had himself experienced in his own short career as a biologist. But even in his role as spokesman for the new scientific elite, he could not escape the nineteenth-century fear of the machine. He had heard Morris speak at Hammersmith; he had discussed *News from Nowhere* in the dissecting room.[1] His earliest imaginative works, the scientific

romances, are symbolic tales in which for Wells, as for
writers throughout the nineteenth century, the machine
is the emblem of modern civilization. And just as Wells
was able to deliver to his son a sermon "in which he
made a great point of monogamy and fidelity,"[2] so too
he was able to argue both sides of the question of progress. In describing technology, Wells often resembles
the narrator of *The War of the Worlds* who, hidden
in the Martian camp and in imminent danger of a particularly unpleasant death, is still fascinated by the
Martian machinery. Even Wells's explicitly anti-utopian
writing describes in detail the advanced technology
brutalizing the proletariat. But to the conventional symbolic use of the machine as metonymy for industrialized
society, Wells, the first scientifically trained writer of
the machine age, adds a further meaning. The machine
becomes the symbol of the specifically scientific mind,
and the scientific romances fables illustrating the inadequacy of pure science divorced from an intuitive
morality. And in continuing the Victorian literary
criticism of pure reason, Wells also continues the
ambivalence toward science itself. For every selfless
investigator of nature's secrets, there is a mad scientist.
The well-intentioned time-explorer is matched by Grif-
fen, the homicidal scientist of the *Invisible Man*.

i

Throughout the nineteenth century, writers had
been attracted to the figure of the scientist-inventor.
With no immediate knowledge of science, however,
they had turned him into a shadowy, symbolic figure;
for Carlyle he was a modern wizard, for Dickens a pa-

thetic example of the need for patent reform.[3] With the exception of George Eliot,[4] Wells is the only nineteenth-century writer who understood science well enough to create psychologically believable scientists. Part of the importance of the early stories and the scientific romances to literary history lies in their widening the range of literature to include the emotional life of the scientist. In so doing, Wells, along with Kipling, is part of a more general movement in the later nineteenth century that sought to bring literature into contact with the new life shaped by the steamship and the airplane and lived by technicians and scientists, as well as poets. But Wells's early short stories never take the machine as hero, as Kipling's do; the protagonist is the scientist himself, and the subject his inner life. In "Argonauts of the Air" (1895), Wells describes the obsession that could drive a man to lose his fortune and finally his life in the vain attempt to invent a flying machine. The hero of "Filmer" (1908) is the inventor of the first airplane, but the emphasis is less on aeronautics than on the somewhat ludicrous psychological conflict between his scientific ambition and his fear of heights. Forced by social pressure to attempt the first flight himself, Filmer commits suicide.

Not only the emotional stress but also the exhilaration of living in the mechanized world become the substance of literature for Wells. The title "scientific romances" resembles Kipling's "romance of the machine," in proclaiming a new literary genre demonstrating that opportunities for courageous action and exotic adventure were not only still possible but actually increased by mechanization. In *Wheels of Chance* (1896), the newly invented bicycle opens up a world of romantic adventure to the young hero. The Victorian visitor to the future in *When the Sleeper Wakes* feels only intense excitement on his first plane ride: "His exhilaration increased rapidly, became a sort of intoxication. He found himself drawing deep breaths of air, laughing aloud, desiring to shout. After a time that desire became too strong for him, and he shouted."[5]

This direct, emotional apprehension of science and technology far outweighs Wells's intellectual understanding of the scientific method itself. By "science," he usually meant only orderly, rational thought; he speaks in his autobiography, for example, of "that urgency for coherence and consistency, that repugnance from haphazard assumptions and arbitrary statements, which is the essential distinction of the educated from the uneducated mind."[6]

For science thus broadly defined, and for the society run in this orderly and efficient manner, the machine appeared to Wells, in his more optimistic moods, as the perfect symbol:

> The plain message physical science has for the world at large is this, that were our political and social and moral devices only as well contrived to their ends as a linotype machine, an antiseptic operating plant, or an electric tramcar, there need now at the present moment be no appreciable toil in the world, and only the smallest fraction of the pain, the fear, and the anxiety that now makes human life so doubtful in its value.[7]

The other legacy of the years at South Kensington was the evolutionary perspective which more than any other influence shapes both the ideas and the form of his response to the machine. Wells acknowledged that his biology course with T. H. Huxley had been "beyond all question, the most educational year"[8] of his life. Huxley had taught that evolution is morally neutral; men must create their own cultivated garden of moral order within an amoral universe. These evolutionary ideas only strengthened Wells's typically Victorian ambivalence to the machine, for it made him see technology as a "given," a social force that can neither be changed nor blamed, only adapted to. And based on the assumption of inevitable technological change, his nonfictional prose could predict the shape of the immediate mechanized future with dispassionate accuracy.

Anticipations (1901), the first of his nonfictional predictions of the future, is based on the common Victorian notion that the railway had been the most important single influence on Victorian life: "The nineteenth century, when it takes its place with the other centuries in the chronological charts of the future, will, if it needs a symbol, almost inevitably have as that symbol a steam engine running upon a railway."[9] The work is a sociological version of the evolutionary method used in the scientific romances; it assumes a continued development of transportation technology and outlines its effects on the future. He predicts, for example, the continued increase in the growth of suburbs, the concentration of capital into massive organizations, persistent unemployment, the "great and expanding body of mechanics and engineers,"[10] and increased government by experts. But unlike the scientific romances, the entire work has the clinical detachment of a doctor describing a chronic condition; it sets out the causes and eventual course of a disease. He provides no cure until *A Modern Utopia* (1905).

A Modern Utopia is the first English utopia to break with the confining literary identification of emotional health with the pastoral life. This utopia is fully mechanized but, unlike other technological utopias such as *The New Atlantis* and *Looking Backward*, its aims are broadly humanistic rather than narrowly utilitarian: "To have free play for one's individuality is, in the modern view, the subjective triumph of existence, as survival in creative work and offspring is its objective triumph."[11] The radically non-Victorian assumption of the book is that these aims of self-development and creative work can be achieved through the increased use of the machine. Always conscious that his life had almost been spent behind a draper's counter, Wells had little sympathy with the Victorian belief in the psychic value of work:

> There is—as in Morris and the outright Return-to-Nature Utopians—a bold make-believe that all toil may be made a joy . . . But indeed this is against all the observed behavior of mankind. It needed the Olympian unworldliness of an irresponsible rich man of the shareholding type, a Ruskin or a Morris playing at life, to imagine as much. Road-making under Mr. Ruskin's auspices was a joy at Oxford no doubt, and a distinction, and it proved the least contagious of practices.[12]

In this utopia, the ability of the machine to eliminate manual labor is seen as a means of freeing the self.

Furthermore, Wells's childhood had shown him enough of the psychological degradation suffered by the poor; here, applied technology produces enough wealth to insure each citizen of the world-state a decent standard of living. Freed from dulling work and the debasement of poverty, the utopians use the new technology as a means of pushing out the limits of their individual growth. Although much of the emotional vitality in the writing depends upon a delight in the wonders of technology, the work does point to the humane ends, albeit generally undefined, for which the machine can be used. The world-wide system of fast, luxurious railways, for example, is praised as a means of expanding the range of experience: "Only the clumsiness of communications limit us now, and every facilitation of locomotion widens not only our potential, but our habitual range."[13]

The work is most convincing in pointing to the aesthetic values of technology. Like Morris and Ruskin, Wells saw artistic activity becoming increasingly necessary to sustain emotional vitality in the machine age, but differed radically in seeing technology itself as the source of this aesthetic satisfaction. With his biologist's sense of function, he saw that the machine could create a new form of beauty: "There is nothing in machinery, there is nothing in embankments and railways and iron bridges and engineering devices to oblige them to be ugly. Ugliness is the measure of imperfection; a thing of human making is for the most part ugly in proportion to the poverty of its constructive thought, to the failure of its producer fully to grasp the purpose of its being."[14] This functionalist theory enabled him to see that, rather than narrowing the province of art, the machine had actually expanded it: "In Utopia a man who designs a tram road will be a cultivated man, an artist craftsman; he will strive as a good writer or a painter strives, to achieve the simplicity of perfection . . . To esteem him a sort of anti-artist, to count every man who makes things with his unaided thumbs an artist, and every man who uses machinery as a brute, is merely a passing phase of human stupidity."[15]

His greatest scorn was directed at the Ruskinians for their equation of art with handwork which relegated creativity to the past. And he never tired of attacking them. In the totally mechanized world of "A Story of the Days to Come" (1897), the heroine is punished for marrying below her class by being compelled to do handwork in a factory based on Ruskinian principles:

> There was a fashion for covering the private apartments of the very wealthy with metal plates beautifully embossed with repeated patterns. The taste of the time demanded, however, that the repetition of the patterns should not be exact—not mechanical, but "natural"—and it was found that the most pleasing arrangement of pattern irregularity was obtained by employing women of refinement and natural taste to punch out the patterns.[16]

Characteristically, however, Wells had mixed feelings even about the handicraft movement. Even though most tasks are mechanized in utopia, there is still work available carving toys by hand from blocks rough-hewn by machine; the narrator notes that goods are often "finished by hand, because the work of unskillful but interested men—and it really is an extremely amusing employment—is found to give a personality and interest to these objects no machine can ever attain."[17]

A Modern Utopia, then, is the mechanized society humanized. Here, the machine rather than regularizing the emotions and obliterating art has become the means of extending the range of human experience and increasing the possibilities of creative activity. In this book, Wells argues that technology can make possible the rich inner life that earlier Victorian writers thought attainable only by insulating the mind from technology. And yet this book is Wells's first statement of humanistic faith in the machine. Before the dispassionate prose of his prophetic writings of 1902-1905, he had written in the scientific romances with less than clinical detachment about the effects of technology on the emotional life. In describing the future, the scientific romances, which, significantly, come to a close with the publication of *A Modern Utopia,* show an ambivalent but predominantly pessimistic picture in which the machine serves as both cause and symbol, not only of social exploitation but of the cruel amorality of the scientific intellect itself.

ii

Within the symbolic mode of Wells's early writings, the machine is quite explicitly made the emblem of modern society. The most representative example is the very early short story, "Lord of the Dynamos" (1894). Here, as throughout Wells's work, the machine is both a metonymy for the immense power of modern technology and a symbol for the amorality of the technologist. The tale sets the scientist against the savage. On one side is Holroyd, the chief of the dynamo-shed who in his combination of efficiency and cruelty epitomizes the Wellsian scientist. His rationality remains untempered by moral teaching*; he "doubted the existence of the Deity but accepted Carnot's cycle."[18] Opposed to Holroyd in the dynamo-shed is Azuma-zi, a superficially civilized Negro of undefined nationality. In the humming dynamo the savage sees a new god, and his religious rites before the machine are the analogue of the more dangerous worship given it by Holroyd who "delivered a theological lecture on the text of his big machine soon after Azuma-zi came . . . 'Look at that . . . Where's your 'eathen idol to match 'im? . . . Kill a hundred men. Twelve per cent. on the ordinary shares . . . and that's something like a Gord.' "[19] Driven mad under his brutal treatment by Holroyd, Azuma-zi sacrifices his enemy to his God by throwing the engineer against an exposed part of the dynamo. His crime is discovered and, about to be captured, he grasps the dynamo himself: "So ended prematurely the worship of the Dynamo Deity, perhaps the most short-lived of all religions. Yet withal it could at least boast a Martyrdom and a Human Sacrifice."[20]

There is little new here in Wells's literary treatment of the dynamo. The machine as evil god appears as far back as Carlyle. And in spite of his scientific train-

---

* Here again is the Huxleyan note. With typical Victorian distrust of reason, Huxley held little faith in the moral efficacy of a scientific education and had even advocated Bible readings in the London schools as a means of ethical training.

ing, Wells still follows the Victorian convention of endowing the machine with a grotesque vitality: "There was the intermittent snorting, panting, and seething of the steam-engines, the suck and thud of their pistons, the dull beat on the air as the spokes of the great driving wheels came round . . . and a fretful tumult from the dynamos."[21] The story is Victorian, too, in seeing the mechanized factory as a microcosm of modern life. Instead of the children of the *Excursion,* or the simple worker such as Stephen Blackpool, in the age of imperialism the savage becomes the example of natural man confronting and being corrupted by the machine. The savage had dreamed of a better life in mechanized England, but, like many Englishmen, had found only the degrading task of caring for the machine. In this microcosm, the dynamos are never quiet; their constant whir makes thought impossible and finally drives Azuma-zi insane. In this world, too, the machine has become more important than man. When Holroyd, its loyal servant, dies, the "scientific manager" hurries to tear his body off the dynamo "for seven or eight trains had stopped midway in the stuffy tunnels of the electric railway."[22]

For Wells, as for Henry Adams, the dynamo had become the symbol of the immense energy available to modern society, and, like Adams, he is concerned with the control of this power. But where he differs from Adams, and from earlier Victorian writers, is in seeing the problem in terms of how scientists themselves, rather than how society in general, can control the machine. The death of Holroyd, whose rationality remains untempered by intuitive morality, suggests the inadequacy of the amoral scientist for this task, and yet the conclusion is typically ambivalent. Equally strong is Wells's fear of how easily the savage can use the machine as an instrument of violence. And for all the implicit criticism of the dispassionate technologist, only the "scientific manager," the representative of the scientific elite whose goal is calm efficiency, can, like Fortinbras, remove the bodies and restore order.

The first and the best scientific romance, *The Time Machine,* also depends on the antimachine conventions of the nineteenth century. Wells accepts the Victorian commonplace that machine-tending is both physically and morally degrading, but instead of using the convention of contemporary realism, as does Dickens or Ruskin, he finds a new form for the old argument in the Butlerian mode of evolutionary fantasy. With an air of scientific credibility, the biological and psychological effects of mechanization are projected into the future in concrete, physical form. The first fictional example of this evolutionary mode is the Morlocks.

And yet this new genre is combined with older conventions of machine literature. Lest the reader miss the connection between the factory and hell, the Morlocks are placed underground, from where, in true diabolic fashion, they emerge during the night to carry off the inhabitants of the upper world. This conventional association of the machine with Hell runs throughout the scientific romances. In *When the Sleeper Wakes,* the entire proletariat is confined to labyrinthine "underways" through which the Victorian visitor is guided like a modern Dante; in *The First Men in the Moon,* the Selenite workers also tend their machines in dark tunnels.

In typical Victorian fashion, Hell is mechanized, paradise is not. The upper world of the Eloi is pictured with all the conventions of the antimachine pastoral; the inhabitants dress in unrestraining garments, eat fruit, dance, and admire the scenery. But Wells is, of course, only setting up the primitivist utopia in order to refute it. The time-traveler, used ironically throughout as a representative but obtuse Victorian mind, is, at first, thoroughly taken in until he is forcefully made to see the inequality and brutalizing machine work on which such Arcadian leisure must subsist. And yet the vapidity which the Eloi display points to the antiaristocratic bias of Wells's criticism and leaves the fable without a positive ideal to offset the mechanized life of the Morlocks. With the humanism that later informs *A Modern Utopia* here satirized, the only virtue seems to be the practical ability of the bustling Victorian visitor to protect the childlike Eloi.

This vision of the future resembles Morris', however, in one respect, in taking its shape from Marxist theory. Wells was first attracted to socialism as a student; he eventually joined the Fabians and remained a member throughout the writing of the scientific romances. In *The Time Machine,* as throughout his early writings, his Darwinism and his Marxism coincide. For the evolutionary fantasy becomes a means not only of expressing the physical and psychological results of mechanization but also of depicting the more generalized effects of the class struggle. In *When the Sleeper Wakes,* the workers of the future, brutalized by centuries of exploitation and mechanized labor, rise in violent rebellion against the ruling class. But if this later work is closer to Morris and Marx in seeing an actual class war in which the proletariat extirpate the bourgeoisie, *The Time Machine* is perhaps more Fabian in having the Morlocks only gradually devour their rulers.

Wells's application of Darwin to the literature of the machine created new figures adequate to the depth of late nineteenth-century pessimism about technological progress. The mental history of the time-traveler, from his elation as he stands at the beginning of a seemingly limitless progress to his final disenchantment, recapitulates the response of the nineteenth century to the machine. On his return, the traveler comments ruefully on his thoughts during his journey into the future, a comment that could apply equally well to a journey from the speed-trial of the Rocket to the present: "What strange developments of humanity, what wonderful advances upon our rudimentary civilization, I thought, might not appear when I came to look nearly into the dim elusive world that raced and fluctuated before my eyes!"[23] For this same disillusionment, Carlyle and Morris had used the conventional mythological figure of Midas; Wells draws his figure from the new science itself, combining the new sense of geologic time with Huxleyan pessimism about the opposition between man and the natural order. The final vision juxtaposing the tiny bicycle-like time machine against giant crabs and silent sea turns the social disenchantment into cosmic pessimism. In Huxleyan terms, even the cultivated garden of civilization carved out of amoral nature by men and machines will be overrun.

The War of the Worlds (1898) continues to criticize mechanization through the literary use of evolutionary figures. The physical grotesqueness of the Martians, like the animality of the Morlocks and the effeminacy of the Eloi, is an evolutionary extrapolation of the present effects of the machine. Wells first used the idea from which the Martians developed in an 1893 magazine article entitled "Man of the Year Million." With *fin-de-siècle* urbanity he explains how the brain must expand, the muscles atrophy as mechanization advances:

> Man now does by wit and machinery and verbal agreement what he once did by bodily toil; for once he had to catch his dinner, capture his wife, run away from his enemies, and continually exercise himself, for love of himself, to perform these duties well. But now all this is changed. Cabs, trains, trams, render speed unnecessary . . . Athleticism takes up time and cripples a man in his competitive examinations, and in business. So is your fleshly man handicapped against his subtler brother. He is unsuccessful in life, does not marry. The better adapted survive.[24]

Only the hand, "the teacher and interpreter of the brain, will become constantly more powerful and subtle as the rest of the musculature dwindles" until the men of the future will have "expanding brains . . . great sensitive hands and diminishing bodies."[25] From these facetious musings, he created the Martians, the emblem of effete mechanized man; observing these flaccid brain cases with gaping mouths and waving tentacles, the narrator comments:

> The perfection of mechanical appliances must ultimately supersede limbs . . . the tendency of natural selection would lie in the direction of their steady diminution through the coming ages . . . We men, with our bicycles and road-skates, our Lilienthal soaring-machines, our guns and sticks and so forth, are just in the beginning of the evolution that the Martians have worked out. They have become practically mere brains, wearing different bodies according to their needs just as men wear suits of clothes and take a bicycle in a hurry or an umbrella in the wet.[26]

The idea expressed here in Wells's usual Darwinian terminology is hardly new. The deterioration of physical strength in a mechanized age was a common fear throughout the century; the Victorian fondness for pastoral utopia depends on the belief that men could use their muscles only when there is no competition from the machine. More specifically, Wells's idea of man as evolving through the development of machines is quite similar to Butler's notion of "machines as limbs," similar enough to suggest, though hardly to prove, that Wells was directly influenced by Butler. Whatever the now unknowable facts of the case may be, Wells was able to do with the evolutionary method what Butler was not, translate intellectual abstractions into the concrete and visible reality of imaginative literature. Just as Morris can turn the abstractions of his essays on art and society into an evocation of the free, sensual life in *News from Nowhere,* so too Wells at his best can, through the evolutionary mode, translate his ideas, which are often Victorian commonplaces, into striking concreteness, as in the transformation of the Victorian fear of physical degeneration into the description of the Martian: "Quasi-muscles abounded in the crab-like handling-machine which, on my first peeping out of the slit, I watched unpacking the cylinder. It seemed infinitely more alive than the actual Martians lying beyond it in the sunset light, panting, stirring ineffectual tentacles, and moving feebly after their vast journey across space."[27]

In the primary action of the book, however, the Martians themselves are forgotten, and the reader is shown a struggle between men and the "fighting machines" the Martians put on to do battle. The battles themselves are a particularly Victorian nightmare, with the fighting machines described in the same figures with which writers had expressed their fears throughout the century. Here, as in *Hard Times,* the machine has become alive and, more explicitly than in earlier literature, master of the earth:

> It was no mere insensate machine driving on its way. Machine it was, with a ringing metallic pace, and long, flexible, glittering tentacles (one of which gripped a young pinetree) swinging and rattling about its strange body. It picked its road as it went striding along, and the brazen hood that surmounted it moved to and fro with the inevitable suggestion of a head looking about.[28]

Within the symbolic mode, the fighting machines are more than the conventional anthropomorphic wonders. In his preceding work, *The Invisible Man* (1897), Wells had illustrated through the naturalistic method the potential for cruelty in the purely scientific intellect; in this work the fighting machines become symbols of this same theme. For the Martians are not evil; they are merely efficient. Their fighting machines are but technologically complex food harvesters. Just as the "melancholy mad elephants" of *Hard Times* represent the amoral logical order of Benthamism, so too the fighting machines symbolize another form of amoral rationality in science. For Wells, as for most nineteenth-century writers, the source of morality is the intuition rather than the intellect; the narrator makes clear the kind of ethical failure for which the Martian machines serve as symbol: "Without the body the brain would, of course, become a mere selfish intelligence, without any of the emotional substratum of the human being."[29]

If for the early Victorian writers the social manifestation of amoral rationality was the factory system, for the late Victorians, Wells and Kipling, it was British imperialism. The Martians use their advanced technology to destroy a civilization of which they are hardly aware; the similarity to British foreign policy in 1898 would have been clear to most readers. This anti-imperialist fable is even told from the viewpoint of the oppressed, with the machine described in typical Wellsian fashion by an outsider rather than an initiate; the narrator says: "I began to compare the things to human machines, to ask myself for the first time in my life how an iron-clad or a steam-engine would seem to an intelligent lower animal."[30] As symbol, then, the machine takes on a political meaning, not only as a metonymy for the new technology that both required and made possible imperialism ("We have got/The Gatling gun and they have not"), but also for the imperialist ethos itself. If the impartiality and dutifulness of the colonial service could be celebrated by the early Kipling through the metaphor of the machine, Wells criticizes this same ethos through the figure of the ruthlessly efficient, thoughtlessly destructive, fighting machines.

For all the symbolic intent, the power of the story lies in its use of ordinary detail within a fantastic frame to create a picture of uncontrolled machinery literally running amuck. The scenes of destruction are effective, too, because they are neither scaled down nor subordinated to the outlines of a plan to control the machine. That Wells in 1898 had no plan to offer is evident in the structure of the fable. For the defeat of the Martians by earthly bacteria does not develop out of the themes of the work; it is only a clever, scientifically credible twist that avoids a pessimistic conclusion. And although the tale ends with the mention of a new world rising from the ruins of the old, the main impression of the work is the ineffectuality of ordinary men before the technological power available to the scientific mind.

The problem of controlling the machine continues into the next scientific romance, *When the Sleeper Wakes* (1899). Although Wells's opinion of it as "one of the most ambitious and least satisfactory"[31] of his works can remain unchallenged, the book does move beyond the Victorian concern with the effect of the machine in the factory to consider the more generalized emotional debilitation within a mechanized world. It is into a future England completely dominated by the machine that the Sleeper, a Victorian gentleman who had fallen into a state of suspended animation, awakes in the year 2100 to find that his fortune has grown through compound interest until he now quite literally owns the world. On being removed from the glass case where he had been kept on public view very much like the Crown Jewels, the gentleman, Graham, finds that the capitalist oligarchy that has run the world corporation in his name is threatened by a proletarian revolution. During an incognito tour of the "underways," the subterranean factories where workers are gradually being turned into Morlocks, he sees the sheer size of mechanized industry overwhelming the workers:

> That walk left on Graham's mind a maze of memories, fluctuating pictures of swathed halls, and crowded vaults seen through clouds of dust, of intricate machines, the racing threads of looms, the heavy beat of stamping machinery, the roar and rattle of belt and armature . . . And everywhere were pillars and cross arching of such a massiveness as Graham had never before seen, thick Titans of greasy, shining brickwork crushed beneath the vast weight of that complex city world, even as these anaemic millions were crushed by its complexity.[32]

The brutalization of the factory worker, the factory as microcosm are all familiar from earlier Victorian writers; what is new in this work is Wells's ability to capture the felt sense of how the mechanized city dulls and confuses the sensibility. Seeing the future world through Graham's eyes, the reader is made to feel the inability of the nineteenth-century mind to adjust to a mechanized environment. This future London, its enclosing glass roof supported by enormous iron pillars, has become a giant Crystal Palace, a fantasia in the iron and glass style of the engineering aesthetic. From the roof, Graham looks down to see how "far below, mere stirring specks and dots, went the people of the unsleeping city in their perpetual daylight, and the moving platforms ran on their incessant journey . . . It was like peering into a gigantic glass hive."[33] But from within, it is a world that can only be perceived fragmentarily:

> His first impression was of overwhelming architecture. The place into which he looked was an aisle of Titanic buildings, curved spaciously in either direction . . . Here and there a gossamer suspension bridge dotted with foot passengers flung across the chasm and the air was webbed with slender cables. A cliff of edifice hung above him, he perceived as he glanced upward, and the opposite façade was grey and dim and broken by great archings, circular perforations, balconies, buttresses, turret projections, myriads of vast windows, and an intricate scheme of architectural relief.[34]

Within this city, Graham feels only his own ineffectuality, an ineffectuality shared by the proletariat. Only Ostrog, the supervisor of the wind vanes that are the source of power for London, can act effectively, and only because he controls the machine. For all his technical skill, for all his strength of character, Ostrog is the typically amoral Wellsian scientist. He turns the revolution to his own purposes and in his self-justifying speech, the machine becomes both cause and symbol of amoral technocracy: "This is the second aristocracy. The real one. Those days of gunpowder and democracy were only an eddy in the stream. The common man now is a helpless unit. In these days we have this great machine of the city, and an organisation complex beyond his understanding."[35]

In the city—powerful, intricate, and impersonal as a machine—the machines themselves acquire a menacing air which serves Wells much as the jungle serves H. Rider Haggard, as a setting providing the atmosphere of danger. For all their symbolic weight, the scientific romances are adaptations of the imperialistic adventure story to the problem of the machine. Wells's heroes are plucky Englishmen who survive their encounters with exotic civilizations, but the strange customs are those of an advanced technological society and the battles are fought amidst sinister machinery rather than exotic flora. The most exciting section of *The Sleeper* is not any discussion of social change but the scene in which the police in their "aeropiles" pursue Graham and his revolutionaries across the great glass roof of London:

> The broad stretch of level before them was a ghastly white, broken only by gigantic masses and moving shapes and lengthy strips of impenetrable darkness, vast ungainly Titans of shadow. All about them, huge metallic structures, iron girders, inhumanly vast as it seemed to him, interlaced, and the edges of wind-wheels, scarcely moving in the lull, passed in great shining curves steeper and steeper up into a luminous haze.[36]

Here the dim shapes of the machine have little symbolic import besides the generalized suggestion of a menacing environment. The machine also functions as a stage setting for scenes of violence in *First Men in the Moon* and *The Time Machine*: "Great shapes like big machines rose out of the dimness, and cast grotesque black shadows, in which dim spectral Morlocks sheltered from the glare."[37]

In the twentieth century, the menacing atmosphere of the factory has not been eliminated, only forgotten; we have even come to accept the metaphor of the machine as the proper figure for society. To most Victorian writers, however, it seemed that the inner life could still remain untouched by the machine; the twentieth-century fear is that the machine will invade even this sanctuary. In emphasizing the potential of the machine to control the mind, Wells's writing moves from the nineteenth into the twentieth century. In the future London, the proletariat knows only what it hears on the "Babble Machine," a gigantic phonograph with an enormous speaking horn. If the technology is quaint, the purpose is not. After the abortive first stage of the revolution, Graham hears the machine in the "underways": "The nearer Babble Machine hooted stupendously, 'Galloop, Galloop,' drowned the end of the sentence, and proceeded in a rather flatter note than before with novel comments on the horrors of disorder. 'Law and order must be maintained,' said the nearer Babble Machine."[38]

The same generalized erosion of emotion is also the main theme of "A Story of the Days to Come" (1897),

Wells's other tale set in the same imaginary London as *The Sleeper*. The plot is the conventional Victorian love story centering on the social problems of marrying outside one's class. Here, the daughter of a prosperous businessman falls in love with and, in spite of family objections, finally marries a mere "flying-stage attendant." Eventually, they sink down into working-class life where, as Wells the social realist shows us, it is difficult for love to survive. Finally, a legacy granted by the girl's jilted fiancé restores them to the happiness of bourgeois life. This most ordinary of plots serves only as a framework within which Wells can describe the dulled sensibility of the present by extrapolating into the future. But for Wells, as for Butler, modern technology has caught up with fantasy, as in this description of the deadening of the sensibility within the ordinary surroundings of the mechanized city:

> For the benefit of those who chanced to be deaf—and deafness was not uncommon in the London of that age, inscriptions of all sizes were thrown from the roof above upon the moving platforms themselves, and on one's hand or on the bald head of the man before one, or on a lady's shoulders, or in a sudden jet of flame before one's feet, the moving finger wrote in unanticipated letters of fire *"'ets r chip t'de,"* or simply *"'ets."* And in spite of all these efforts so high was the pitch at which the city lived, so trained became one's eyes and ears to ignore all sorts of advertisement, that many a citizen had passed that place thousands of times and was still unaware of the existence of the Suzannah Hat Syndicate.[39]

And beyond the bombarding sensations of the street,

there still stands the mechanized factory, watched over by the same sacrificial god of the machine that appears throughout nineteenth-century literature:

> Denton's [job] was to mind a complicated hydraulic press that seemed almost an intelligent thing . . . The most salient fact to his mind was that it had to be conducted in ruby light, and as a consequence the room in which he worked was lit by one coloured globe that poured a lurid and painful illumination about the room. In the darkest corner stood the press whose servant Denton had now become: it was a huge, dim, glittering thing with a projecting hood that had a remote resemblance to a bowed head, and, squatting like some metal Buddha in this weird light that ministered to its needs, it seemed to Denton . . . almost as if this must needs be the obscure idol to which humanity in some strange aberration had offered up his life.[40]

Unlike earlier Victorian writers, however, Wells does not contrast the mechanized world to the emotional freedom of a more primitive life. For Wells, the factory and advertising are the necessary conditions of modern life, and he never tires of attacking those who would take the pastoral ideal literally. Here the lovers, feeling, like any Victorians, that romance cannot survive in the machine age, flee to the countryside which, in the twenty-second century, is inhabited only during the day by the commuting workers of the Food Company. In a heavy-handed satire that anticipates E. M. Forster's far more subtle "The Machine Stops," Wells describes how people accustomed to being tended by machinery cannot withstand the rigors of the simple life. Bored, chilled by the rain, their innocence shattered in this false Eden, the Adam and Eve of the future return to the city. In heavy Miltonic tone, Wells suggests that the knowledge of the machine, much like the knowledge of good and evil, has irrevocably expelled men from the garden: "Silently, side by side, they went across the empty garden-space into the old high road, and set their faces resolutely towards the distant city—towards the complex mechanical city of those latter days, the city that had swallowed up mankind."[41]

And yet, for all the intensity with which the emotional cost of mechanization is described, the story takes on a curious ambiguity as Wells switches between imaginative writer and scientist-prophet. The impersonality of a descriptive statement such as "he lived in a vast hotel near that part of London called Seventh Way, and had very large and comfortable apartments on the seventeenth floor. Households and family life had long since disappeared with the progressive refinement of manners,"[42] does not indicate whether Wells is lamenting the decline of domesticity or praising the increase in efficiency. And yet this ambiguity is functional here in enabling Wells to describe life in a mechanized society without having to make a judgment about technological progress. And here, as in *The War of the Worlds*, the final turn of plot, in its optimism, contradicts the fear of the machine pervading the story. As in much Victorian fiction, the final legacy enables the protagonist to live happily ever after within the society that has been criticized throughout the work.

The reluctance to acknowledge the pessimistic conclusion suggested by the descriptions of mechanization also mars *The Sleeper*. In the final episode, the airplane is both the means of bringing the savage "black police" from Africa and, under Graham's control, the instrument for saving the proletarian revolution. But during the final air battle, Graham, the moral leader who might have controlled technology, is killed. In his preface to the revised edition, Wells attempts to clarify the ending, but his explicit statement is quite as ambiguous as the book itself. He notes that he eliminated "certain dishonest and regrettable suggestions that the People beat Ostrog. My Graham dies, as all his kind must die, with no certainty of either victory or defeat."[43]

In *The First Men in the Moon*, any ambiguity about control of the machine dissolves before open criticism of the purely rational scientist. The use of first person narrative here, as in *The Sleeper*, again conveys the perplexity of the average nineteenth-century man before mechanized complexity. The young man who tells the story receives only dissociated impressions of the machinery:

> [There] was a vast mass of machinery in active movement, whose flying and whirling parts were visible indistinctly . . . The meaning and structure of this huge apparatus I cannot explain, because we neither of us learnt what it was for or how it worked . . . At first the thing seemed only reasonably large and near to us; and then I saw how exceedingly little the Selenites upon it seemed, and I realized the full immensity of cavern and machine.[44]

But to this adventure story among the machines is added an epilogue criticizing the scientist for his inability to comprehend the emotional effects of mechanization. This takes the form of a series of broadcasts from the moon by Cavor, the inventor of the anti-gravity propellant, who has accidentally been left behind. This epitome of the amoral Wellsian scientist had been drawn earlier by comparison with a machine: "When he said it was 'the most important' research the world had ever seen he simply meant it squared up so many theories, settled so much that was in doubt; he had troubled no more about the application of the stuff he was going to turn out than if he had been a machine that makes guns."[45] In Cavor's description of mechanized life among the Selenites, the Swiftian disparity between his admiration and the destructive process he is describing points, as well as any realistic description of factory life and factory owners, not only to the psychic danger of specialization but to the limitations of pure reason:

> The bulk of these insects, however, who go to and fro upon the spiral ways . . . are, I gather, of the operative class. "Machine hands," indeed some of these are in actual fact—it is no figure of speech; the single tentacle of the moon-calf hind is replaced by huge single or paired bunches of three, or five, or seven digits for clawing, lifting, guiding, the rest of them no more than subordinate appendages to these important parts . . .
> The making of these various sorts of operative must be a very curious and interesting process . . . Quite recently I came upon a number of young Selenites, confined in jars from which only the fore limbs pro-

truded, who were being compressed to become machine-minders of a special sort. The extended "hand" in this highly developed system of technical education is stimulated by irritants and nourished by injection while the rest of the body is starved . . . That wretched-looking hand sticking out of its jar seemed to appeal for lost possibilities; it haunts me still, although, of course, it is really in the end a far more humane proceeding than our earthly method of leaving children to grow into human beings, and then making machines of them.[46]

In keeping with the attack on rationalism, Wells shows the ruler of the Selenite Kingdom, the Grand Lunar, as having evolved, like the Martians, into a being of virtually pure brain. This creature of atrophied limbs and enormous braincase, along with his attendant specialized intellectuals (one has been bred as a living memory, another as a walking calculator), rules the moon with an efficiency that Cavor can only admire. But for Wells, this rationalism is totally heartless, the physical distortion a sign of the emotional distortion demanded by the goal of technological efficiency. And as an emblem of this society Wells, here at his most pessimistic, uses the machine. Admiringly, Cavor the scientist tells the earth that the thoughts of the typical lunar herdsman "are of mooncalf pastures, and his dialect an accomplished mooncalf technique. So also he loves his work, and discharges in perfect happiness the duty that justifies his being. And so it is with all sorts and conditions of Selenites—each is a perfect unit in a world machine."[47]

After *The First Men in the Moon*, Wells turned

to more straightforward exposition of his ideas, producing within three years *Anticipations* (1901) and
Mankind in the Making (1903). When he returned to
the scientific romance with *The Food of the Gods* in
1904, the prophet had taken over from the artist. If, in
The First Men in the Moon, the social fable is still
only appended to the adventure story, this tale of the
ramifying effect of a chemical that increases the size of
all living things is pure allegory throughout. As Wells
notes in his *Experiment in Autobiography*, "the idea
of a change in scale as a matter of quite vital importance in human experience had gained a footing in
my brain and was stirring about there, and since it
could find no adequate outlet in any modification of
Fabian policy, it expressed itself in a fantastic story,
The Food of the Gods."[48]

The idea of increased scale, of larger machinery,
larger buildings, larger social units is not new to Wells;
it is seen throughout the scientific romances, in the
workers being figuratively crushed by the weight of
mechanized industry in *The Sleeper*, in the menacing
size of the machinery in the tunnels of the moon. In
this last scientific romance, the figure of the ordinary
man dwarfed by the machine also appears; visiting his
giant sons, the father of the new race "followed a
steeply descending way that passed beneath an arch of
interlocking machinery, and so came to the bottom of
the pit. This gangway, wide and vacant, and yet rela-
tively narrow, conspired with everything about it to
enhance Redwood's sense of his own littleness."[49] But
what is new in this tale is that for the first time the

ambivalence about the machine has disappeared. Technological progress is no longer merely inevitable, but wholly beneficial. The work suggests that the giant children with their "monstrous wheeled machine,"[50] their wind vanes, and "great engines"[51] are unjustly and foolishly feared by the "little people." This change from ambivalence to enthusiasm has occurred because for the first time Wells introduces his plan for controlling technology, the idea of a ruling elite. The allegorical figures for this elite are children, rather than scientists, thus suggesting the limitations of rationalistic education and the necessity of keeping undistorted the instinctive moral sense.

With the introduction of the thesis that control of the machine must pass to an elite, the scientific romances necessarily come to an end. For the conflict at their center, the struggle of ordinary man against amoral technocracy, a conflict represented by the physical battles between Victorian adventurers and machinery symbolizing this amoral rationality, has been resolved. And Wells could move from the province of imaginative literature, the rendering of conflict, to social planning. Indeed, the notion of an elite demands some explication, for, as Anthony West notes, in *Food of the Gods* Wells seems to evade his deep seated pessimism by positing a change in human nature as the prerequisite for utopia.[52] The fable gives no reason for the giant childrens' morality; the giant rats, fed on the same chemical, are hardly more virtuous than their ancestors.

His next book, *A Modern Utopia*, is devoted to

proving in specific terms that a ruling elite is indeed possible in this world and that moral control can thus be established over technological power. With the typical Victorian faith in education, Wells dwells at great length on the practical details of training and sustaining the Samurai. In keeping with his distrust of reason, the emphasis throughout is on moral rather than scientific training. Theirs is to be a noble asceticism, their moral sense to be renewed not by technical training but by communion with the self on solitary trips and an almost Wordsworthian communication with a transcendent power.

Through this faith in modern philosopher kings, Wells could still delight in technological progress and, for a time, overcome his awareness of its dangers. But the hope of such an elite is contradicted not only by the experience of history, but by Wells's own deep sense of human evil which gives the scientific romances so much of their power. Although he had described the depths of human animality in *The Island of Dr. Moreau* and the cruelty of pure reason in *The War of the Worlds*, he nevertheless repressed this awareness to put his trust in the ability of an elite to handle wisely the power of the machine. Only at the very end of his life, after the horrors of two world wars, did he return to the vision of the scientific romances: "Spread out and examine the pattern of events, and you will find yourself face to face with a new scheme of being, hitherto unimaginable by the human mind . . . The writer is convinced that there is no way out or round or through the impasse. It is the end."[53]

7   The Romance of the Machine: *Rudyard Kipling*

In the first year of the nineteenth century, Wordsworth optimistically predicted that

> if the labours of Men of science should ever create any material revolution, direct or indirect, in our condition, and in the impressions which we habitually receive, the Poet will sleep then no more than at present; he will be ready to follow the steps of the Man of science, not only in those general indirect effects, but he will be at his side, carrying sensation into the midst of the objects of the science itself.[1]

But if the nineteenth-century writer did follow the "Men of science," the chief sensation he carried was deep concern at the pace. It was not until the end of the century that there emerged a literature intended to carry the sensation of enthusiasm "into the midst of the objects of the science itself," a literature that, taking the machine as its subject, took the vocabulary of the technician and the engineer as its language in order to communicate the "feel" of the new technology that had

replaced "rocks and stones and trees" as the natural
surroundings of the modern Englishman. Of this late
nineteenth-century literary movement, which includes
the work of W. E. Henley and John Davidson, Kipling
is the most successful representative. While his desire to
become a "Robbie Burns to sing the Song o' Steam"
made him appear to many somewhat coarse, somewhat
like a locomotive engineer talking shop during a gathering at D. G. Rossetti's, his work points toward a new
idiom and a new social realism that anticipates much in
twentieth-century poetry. And yet his attempt to create
a literature of the machine is continually undercut by a
typically Victorian ambivalence until, in the last stage
of his career, his writing returns to the antimachine
modes of the nineteenth century.

i

If Kipling had remained in India, it is unlikely that
he would have been tempted to create a literature of
the machine. His rare newspaper descriptions of technology in India, like Dickens' journalistic pieces on the
machine, are written in the manner of the technological
grotesque, with little concern for social criticism or
symbolic meaning. Personified locomotives "adorn
themselves with red lead, and leer like decayed beauties;
and in the Jamalpur works there is no escape from
them."[2] Still, beneath this facetiousness are signs of the
awe at technological power that will inform his later
writing; he describes the deserted repair shed: "The
silence is the weirdest touch of all. Some sprightly soul
. . . has daubed in red lead on the end of an iron toolbox
a caricature of some friend who is evidently a riveter.

The picture has all the interest of an Egyptian car-touche, for it shows that men have been here, and that the engines do not have it all their own way."[3] And yet the railway town of Jamalpur was an exotic Western growth that needed elaborate care to survive in this primitive land. It was only on his journey to London at the age of twenty-four that he suddenly confronted the full power of modern technology, in the locomotives driving across the great mountain ranges of the United States and the steamship cutting across the oceans.[4]

The stories written during this first enchantment with the mechanized European world Kipling collected under the properly Calvinistic title *The Day's Work* (1898). Although the tales celebrate engineers and machinery, the volume is infused with Kipling's own ambivalence to the machine, a feeling caused in part by his reservations about the social benefits of technology and in part by a questioning of the philosophical materialism of science itself. In *The Day's Work* both the opening story, "The Bridge-Builders," and the conclud-ing one, "Brushwood Boy," set the accomplishments of men and machines against the dimly apprehended op-eration of transcendental forces.

In "The Bridge-Builders," the suggestions of trans-cendental power point to a theme central to Kipling, as to many Victorian writers, the limitations of the scien-tific mind. The hero, Findlayson, is a British engineer supervising the construction of a bridge he himself de-signed to span the Ganges. The story begins with praise for the material strength of the bridge and the mental immovability of its creator: "For three years he had endured heat and cold, disappointment, discomfort, danger, and disease, with responsibility almost too heavy for one pair of shoulders; and day by day, through that time, the great Kashi Bridge over the Ganges had grown under his charge."[5] But as a flood comes to test the nearly completed work, the tale moves into another dimension. Having absent mindedly taken some opium, Findlayson soon feels himself adrift on the swollen river, cast upon an island and privy to a discussion of his bridge by Hindu deities incarnated as animals.

In its very form, this dream vision implicitly criticizes the assumptions of both science and Empire. The "realistic" section of the tale turns Findlayson, the Victorian ideal of engineer as hero, into a new god; he looks upon his bridge "and with a sigh of contentment saw that his work was good . . . his bridge, raw and ugly as original sin, but *pukka*—permanent—to endure when all memory of the builder—even of the splendid Findlayson truss—had perished."[6] The dream vision does not reject engineering skill; it only points to its limited importance in an essentially spiritual world. For Kipling, as for Carlyle, the transcendental perspective serves to reconcile vitalism to the fact of machinery. The spirit of the Ganges places the technological feat in a transcendental context: "Does Mother Gunga die, then, in a year, that she is so anxious to see vengeance now? The deep sea was where she runs but yesterday, and to-morrow the sea shall cover her again as the Gods count that which men call time. Can any say that this their bridge endures till to-morrow?"[7]

Furthermore, this dream vision, whose reality is

always ambiguous, is the perfect vehicle for suggesting, but not asserting, doubts about the more tangible effects of the machine on Indian life. Even the debate among the gods is unresolved. Considering the effect of technological progress on religious faith, a common Victorian theme, Krishna says that the spread of materialistic thought is inevitable, but a lesser god, with a touch of dramatic irony, is given a more Whiggish position: "The fire-carriages move one by one, and each bears a thousand pilgrims. They do not come afoot any more, but rolling upon wheels, and my honour is increased."[8] Another god points out other, less than beneficent effects of the Indian railway system: "Who smote at Puri, under the Image there, her thousands in a day and a night, and bound the sickness to the wheels of the fire-carriages, so that it ran from one end of the land to the other? . . . The fire-carriages have served thee well, Mother of Death."[9] And the Elephant God points to the economic motive, to which Kipling was not blind, behind the English love of fire-carriages:

> It is for the profit of my *mahajuns*—my fat money-lenders that worship me at each new year, when they draw my image at the head of the account-books. I, looking over their shoulders by lamplight, see that the names in the books are those of men in far places—for all the towns are drawn together by the fire-carriage, and the money comes and goes swiftly, and the account-books grow as fat as—myself.[10]

Finally, Indra, Father of the Gods, concludes the debate, not by any explicit judgment of the machine, but by setting both technological progress and Empire against

the eternality of the transcendent: "When Brahm ceases
to dream, the Heavens and the Hells and Earth dis-
appear . . . The dreams come and go, and the nature of
the dreams changes, but still Brahm dreams."[11] Even
the resolution of the plot is ambivalent. Like King
Arthur in Tennyson's idyll of "The Holy Grail,"
Findlayson shakes off his visionary experiences to return
to work.

   In his early stories, then, the object of criticism is
not technology itself but the proud self-sufficiency of
a rationalism which is symbolized by the machine. And
to accept technology while rejecting scientific rationalism, Kipling, like Carlyle, transforms the machine into
the embodiment of spiritual forces rather than of
deterministic natural laws. In "Wireless" (1902), the
main character is a reincarnation of Keats; he is a young
druggist suffering from consumption and in love with a
girl named Fanny Brand. One cold night, the narrator
sees the druggist fall into a trance and write some dis-
jointed snatches of "The Eve of Saint Agnes." The
narrator then walks into a second room where another
young man, experimenting with new Marconi equipment, has been receiving jumbled messages from two
ships at sea rather than from the expected sender. The
radio operator speaks for Kipling in associating these
new technological phenomena not with the physical
sciences, but with spiritualism: "Have you ever seen a
spiritualistic seance? It reminds me of that sometimes—
odds and ends of messages coming out of nowhere—a
word here and there—no good at all."[12] Wells's contemporaneous scientific romances also depend for their

effect on the general mystery surrounding science, but with Wells there is always an effort, albeit often fanciful, to give the stories a scientific credibility. Kipling's point, however, is that for all its practical technological achievement, science is an insufficient means of explaining the essentially vitalistic qualities of nature. The wisest figure in the story is the radio experimenter, the technically competent man aware of the limitations of technology; he says of his equipment: "That is the thing that will reveal to us the Powers—whatever the Powers may be—at work—through space—a long distance away."[13] And the object of ridicule is the rationalist, the druggist himself who, unaware that he has received "messages coming out of nowhere," comments: "Mediums are all imposters."[14]

For all the reservations created by his transcendentalism, the machine still became for Kipling, more than for any other major nineteenth-century writer, a literary figure for that which he held most valuable. For the psychological reasons behind this atypical literary use of the machine, Edmund Wilson's analysis of Kipling's mind is still the best source.[15] As Wilson suggests, Kipling sought to defend himself against the vagaries of his own mind and the threats of external enemies by seeking a severe emotional discipline, which he found in a complete identification with Empire. And since the machine had become a conventional symbol for emotional restraint, and for the polity that demands such restraint, it became for Kipling charged with positive associations.

To exemplify this belief in the orderly machine as

the ideal of psychic life, Kipling created an entirely new
literary form in which the personified machine is itself
the hero. The "Ship That Found Herself" (1895) is a
thinly veiled moral and psychological fable in which a
steamship succeeds as it becomes, to use the conventional nineteenth-century terms, less human and more
mechanical. The individual parts of the ship, the rivets,
the deck beams, the stern, like the different parts of the
body in the traditional story, each complains that it
alone keeps the ship afloat. Finally, after a storm, each
part realizes that it can survive only by subordinating
itself to the concerted action of the whole. By the end
of the voyage, the strongly individual personalities of
each separate part have been silenced, fused into the
stable, ordered state that Kipling saw exemplified by the
machine: "When a ship finds herself all the talking of
the separate pieces ceases and melts into one voice,
which is the Soul of the Ship."[16] The point of this simple
parable is emphasized in the introductory poem in
which the loss of self is celebrated in the activity of the
marine engine:

> We now, held in captivity,
> Spring to our labour nor grieve!
> See now, how it is blesseder,
> Brothers, to give than receive!
> Keep trust, wherefore ye were made,
> Paying the duty ye owe;
> For a clean thrust and the shear of the blade
> Will carry us where we would go.[17]

Kipling used the engine often as a symbol of perfect obedience, for the machine is true not only to the

laws of nature but to its immediate superior, the engineer. "The Secret of the Machines," as celebrated in the poem of that name, is that the machine can function in rigid compliance to the law, unencumbered by human emotion; the verse could equally well celebrate Kipling's ideal colonial officer:

> But remember, please, the Law by which we live,
> We are not built to comprehend a lie,
> We can neither love nor pity nor forgive.
> If you make a slip in handling us you die![18]

Losing one's identity is often exceptionally pleasant, and Kipling's writings shine with the joy of belonging. In his own life he gloried in his adoption by the Royal Navy and his initiation into their technical secrets. A letter of 1897 describing the trial-run of a new destroyer shows not only his boyish enthusiasm—"It took me two days to get the 'jumps' out of my legs. But I wouldn't have missed the trip for anything"—but also the same use of technological jargon as a sign of initiation that muddies his more public prose: "Two engines of 3,000 h.p. apiece were making about 230 to the minute—maybe a trifle less."[19] This delight in belonging, Kipling objectified in another tale of personified machines, ".007." The protagonist, who bears little relation to the modern hero of the same name, is a young locomotive that longs to be accepted by the older engines on the line. Not until he proves himself by speeding a wrecking-crew to the site of a crash is he accepted by his superiors. But in spite of the serious intent of this and other tales of personified machines, such attempts to create a literature for the machine age by taking the machine as protagonist are bound to fail. Working from the assumption that the ideal mind should resemble a machine, Kipling strips from his machine-heroes the impulsiveness and variety that, as other Victorian writers suggested, distinguishes human from mechanical activity. Because of this inherent simplification, the literature of personified machines survives only in children's books.[20]

Again suggesting discipline and submission, the machine also became for Kipling the figure for an ideal social order. In the Indian Civil Service, in the cavalry columns on the veldt, in the Channel Fleet, self-development and individual opinion were to be sacrificed to the state. If Morris is typical of most Victorian writers in opposing the regimentation of mechanized society to the emotional freedom of a primitive social order, Kipling, fearful of this same emotional energy, accepts the modern machine itself as the social paradigm. McAndrew, the Scottish ship's engineer, points to the giant marine engines: "Now, a' together, hear them lift their lesson—theirs an' mine:/'Law, Orrder, Duty an' Restraint, Obedience, Discipline!' "[21]

For Kipling, as for other nineteenth-century writers, the machine had become the emblem of modern society. But whereas most writers attacked the Whiggish assumptions of their age by showing the machine in terms of destructive energy, Kipling described the machine as turned to constructive purposes. When McAndrew sees his life sanctified by his tending of the engines—"Think not I dare to justify myself before the

Lord,/But—average fifteen hunder souls safe-borne fra'
port to port"[22]—this Scotch Calvinist is a latter-day
Carlyle, celebrating the new technology under the older
doctrine of work. And like Carlyle, Kipling is so en-
tranced by the idea of work that he seldom notices the
worker:

> From forge and farm and mine and bench,
> Deck, altar, outpost lone—
> Mill, school, battalion, counter, trench,
> Rail, senate, sheepfold, throne—
> Creation's cry goes up on high
> From age to cheated age:
> "Send us the men who do the work
> "For which they draw the wage!"[23]

In his pre-World War I writing, there is no mention of
the emotional effect of mechanized labor. And in Kipling is explicit what was only suggested in Carlyle, technological progress exported as a civilizing imperial
mission. One example of Kipling's equation of technological progress with Empire will serve for many:

> Keep ye the Law—be swift in all obedience—
> Clear the land of evil, drive the road and bridge
>   the ford.
> Make ye sure to each his own
> That he reap where he hath sown;
> By the peace among Our peoples let men know
>   we serve the Lord![24]

Protecting the Empire, securing the blessings of
Progress, was the Royal Navy, its power continually increasing through technology. Although Kipling knew
war too well to love it for its own sake (some of his war

stories are as bitterly realistic as any modern war literature), he saw England's wars, like its Empire, as funda-
mentally righteous and the machine as the instrument
of this righteousness. In his poetry of World War I, his
praise of the machine itself, like the paean to the
destroyer in the unfortunately affirmative conclusion of
Wells's *Tono Bungay* and like the praise of jet planes in
modern war literature, only serves to ennoble warfare
by evading the fact of human suffering. Again the
personification of the machine only creates a literature
inadequate to the complexity of human emotion. In
"Tin Fish," for example, the song of the efficient tor-
pedoes neglects entirely the suffering of the victims:

> The ships destroy us above
> And ensnare us beneath.
> We arise, we lie down, and we move
> In the belly of Death.
>
> The ships have a thousand eyes
> To mark where we come . . .
> But the mirth of a seaport dies
> When our blow gets home.[25]

Only in the stories written after World War I does the
focus shift from military technology per se to its effect
on the mind.

Before World War I, Kipling's only treatment of
the psychological effect of technology comes in the
curious fantasy, "As Easy as A.B.C." (1907). This Wellsian extrapolation of the present effects of technology
into the future appears on the surface to be another
fable in praise of authoritarianism. Set in the twenty-
first century with the world governed by the "Aerial

Board of Control," the story celebrates the efficiency of the A.B.C. in stifling an outbreak of "democracy" in the American village of Chicago. In describing the ability of the air armada to protect the advocates of majority rule from a justifiably enraged populace, the story seems to delight, as do so many of Kipling's stories, in the repressive use of technological power. Describing a new weapon that subdues through blinding light and maddening sound, the narrator says: "We descended by the stairs, to find ourselves knee-deep in a grovelling crowd, some crying that they were blind, others beseeching us not to make any more noises, but the greater part writhing face downward, their hands or caps before their eyes."[26] And yet, for all the implicit praise of violence, there is also the suggestion of the anguish created in the sensitive man forced to witness this destructive power: " 'Ah no! No!' cried Dragomiroff [a scientist] at my side. I could feel the old man tremble. 'I do not know all that you can do, but be kind! I ask you to be a little kind to them below! This is horrible— horrible.' "[27] The healing of minds shattered by such mechanized warfare was to become the central theme of his post-World War I writing.

It is in describing the quality of life beyond the political structure that Kipling most strongly suggests the emotional debilitation created by technological progress. An earlier story set in the same future of air travel under A.B.C. control, "With the Night Mail," can praise technocracy for creating a mechanized Pax Britannica only because it concentrates on the heroic adventures of the fliers themselves. This later tale, which, like Wells's best fantasies, tries to envision the temper of life within a totally mechanized society, strongly suggests a resultant decay in psychic energy. This *fin-de-siècle* sense of ennervation is established in the first paragraph: "One knows that easy communications nowadays, and lack of privacy in the past, have killed all curiosity among mankind, but as the Board's Official Reporter I am bound to tell my tale."[28] And throughout, the story follows the primitivistic theme in its criticism of the machine; like Morris, Kipling sees mechanized society as increasingly effete, increasingly isolated from what is natural and organic. Here men sleep eleven hours out of twenty-four, and the birth rate is rapidly falling. If reality is to be identified with the rhythms of organic life, this reality is becoming increasingly unknowable: "It came out as we sat over breakfast, that, with the exception of Arnott and Pirolo, none of us had ever seen a corpse, or knew in what manner the spirit passes."[29]

ii

Because, for Kipling, the machine seemed a providential means of bearing the white man's burden, his delight in the machine was far greater than that of most nineteenth-century writers. And he set out to create a literature that would express this wonder and admiration. His is the first major attempt in English literature to create a literary mode that would draw not only its subject matter but its very language from the fact of mechanization. And if Kipling had himself in mind when he asked for a new "Robbie Burns" to "sing the

Song o' Steam," the choice of Burns is significant, for it suggests his vision of himself as the untutored bard bringing in a new romanticism for the machine age. His specific variety of romanticism can be defined as the periodic revolution in literature that casts out the literary conventions no longer suited to a new perception of the world. The earlier nineteenth-century writers had tried to deal with the new sights and the new emotions of mechanized life with conventions, like the pastoral and the sublime, that had become inapplicable to the world of factories and steam engines. Kipling's purpose, like that of Stephen Spender and C. Day Lewis later in the twentieth century, was to bring literature closer to contemporary experience by developing new literary forms that could include the fact of the machine.

In this attempt, Kipling's intentions, and his problems, parallel those of the earlier romantic poets. Coleridge writes in the *Biographia Literaria:*

> Mr. Wordsworth . . . was to propose to himself as his object, to give the charm of novelty to things of every day, and to excite a feeling analogous to the supernatural, by awakening the mind's attention from the lethargy of custom, and directing it to the loveliness and the wonders of the world before us; an inexhaustible treasure, but for which, in consequence of the film of familiarity and selfish solicitude we have eyes, yet see not, ears that hear not, and hearts that neither feel nor understand.[30]

But if at the beginning of the nineteenth century the "things of every day" were, for Wordsworth at least, the primitive and rural, at the end of the century they were, as Kipling saw, the mechanized and urban. And if Wordsworth, directing attention to the "loveliness and the wonders of the world before us," pictured the yet unspoiled Cumberland hills, Kipling pointed to the express train and the steamship.

For both a revolution in sensibility demanded a revolution in language. To Kipling it seemed time to cast out the Keatsian prettiness intended to provide an escape from mechanized life in favor of a language that would express the new occupations and new perceptions of the machine age. Just as Burns celebrated rural Scottish life with the diction of the people themselves, so Kipling saw himself as coming closer to the "real language of men" by using in literature the language of the engineer. In his writing, this radical literary theory is expressed most explicitly not by a poet, but by a ship's engineer; McAndrew says:

> Romance! Those first-class passengers they like it
> very well,
> Printed an' bound in little books; but why don't
> poets tell?
> I'm sick of all their quirks an' turns—the loves an'
> doves they dream—
> Lord, send a man like Robbie Burns to sing the
> Song o' Steam![31]

In looking to a "realistic" poetry celebrating the machine, Kipling is part of a more general movement in turn-of-the-century poetry. W. E. Henley, who had drawn the young Kipling into his circle, wrote his hymn to the machine in "A Song of Speed." This poem, which, like the description of Dombey's train ride, tries to reproduce the new rhythms of the machine age in the meter, is addressed to a Mercedes touring car. But it is impossible even for Henley to dwell on the car as an object worthy of poetry in itself; like earlier writers, he must transform the machine into symbol. Here, the speed of the car becomes a sign of worship through work, and the automobile, rather than the "ringing grooves of change," a figure equating technological progress with Divine Providence:

> And at times, when He feels
> That His creatures are doing
> Their best to assert
> Their part in His dream,
> He loosens His fist
> And a miracle slips from it
> Into the hands
> Of His adepts and servants . . .
> Thus hath He slackened
> His grasp, and this Thing,
> This marvellous Mercedes,
> This triumphing contrivance,
> Comes to make other
> Man's life than she found it:
> The Earth for her tyres
> As the Sea for his keels.[32]

As a poet of the machine, John Davidson, also a member of Henley's circle, is far more successful than Henley. His "Testament of Sir Simon Simplex Concerning Automobilism" also praises the automobile, but by "placing" through the use of dramatic monologue the work moves beyond the simple praise of technology to become a psychological study of how the personal quest for power can be expressed through the machine. His other machine poetry is far more conventional; the railway station is not an object of beauty in itself but a symbol for the repressiveness of mechanized urban life; it is the tenor rather than the vehicle of metaphor:

> . . . delta wide of platforms, whence
> Discharges into London's sea, immense
> And turbulent, a brimming human flood,
> A river inexhaustible of blood
> That turns the wheels.[33]

But if this turn-of-the-century movement toward a poetry of the machine did not develop into a major genre, part of the reason lies in the inherent difficulties in writing poetry dealing with mechanization. Kipling's failure to achieve his poetic ends will serve to illustrate some of these problems.

For all his desire to create a new literary form, Kipling still worked most often in the typical nineteenth-century manner by applying old conventions to the new subject matter of technology. In order to arouse the reader from the "lethargy of custom" and direct his attention, in Coleridge's terms, to "the loveliness and the wonders" of modern technology, he often uses a lush Pre-Raphaelite diction. He describes "The Deep-Sea Cables":

> There is no sound, no echo of sound, in the deserts
> of the deep,
> Or the great grey level plains of ooze where the
> shell-blurred cables creep.
>
> Here in the womb of the world—here on the tie-
> ribs of earth

> Words, and the words of men, flicker and flutter
> and beat.[34]

But most commonly, Kipling, like Wells, attempts to convey the excitement of the mechanized world through the adventure story. In applying the term "romance" to the machine, Kipling is using the word in the same sense as his contemporaries, Joseph Conrad and Robert Louis Stevenson. Of course, the use of the technological adventure story is in itself an implicit refutation of nineteenth-century writers, such as Morris, who stressed the debilitating effects of mechanization in the present by contrasting it to an heroic past. The main theme in Kipling's tales of the machine is that calm, manly courage is still demanded by mechanized work. When a passenger asks McAndrew whether steam "spoils romance at sea," the engineer replies by describing the new forms of danger faced by the technician: "I'd been doon that morn to see what ailed the throws,/Man-holin', on my back—the cranks three inches off my nose."[35] When, in Kipling's best-known lines on the machine, "all unseen,/Romance brought up the nine-fifteen," it is a romance defined in terms of danger overcome through physical courage:

> His hand was on the lever laid,
> His oil-can soothed the worrying cranks,
> His whistle waked the snowbound grade,
> His fog-horn cut the reeking Banks;
> By dock and deep and mine and mill
> The Boy-god reckless laboured still![36]

The celebration of courage and skill informs his technological adventure stories as much as it does his

tales of the Khyber Pass. In "With the Night Mail,"
one of his most popular tales, the conventional sea story
is only thinly disguised by the technological trappings.
The pilot, described as having the "brooding sheathed
glance characteristic of eagles and aeronauts," could
be any Elizabethan sea dog as he waits in "the Captains'
Room (this wakes an echo of old romance)."[37] The
danger encountered during the flight is an electrical
storm rather than the conventional typhoon, and it is
overcome by the steadiness of the captain and the crew.
His poems on freighters and their crews are set in the
form of ballads, as if to emphasize that the primary facts
of courage and death persist into the mechanized present. The "Ballad of the 'Bolivar'" (1890), describing
the hazardous voyage of a leaky tramp steamer, could
very well have occurred on a leaky sailing ship:

> Just a pack o' rotten plates puttied up with tar,
> In we came, an' time enough, 'cross Bilbao Bar.
> Overloaded, undermanned, meant to founder, we
> Euchred God Almighty's storm, bluffed the Eternal
> Sea![38]

Without the symbolic density found in Wells, the
technological adventure story fails because although its
subject is technology, its effect is to deny the influence
of technological change. For a literature of the machine
that dwells upon physical heroism held little relevance
to Kipling's time and even less to our own. Even though
some mechanized tasks require physical courage, most
do not; there are only a few astronauts and many space
scientists. And by emphasizing the persistence of the
heroic virtues, Kipling is denying the very real psy-

chological, as well as social, changes created by the machine. If literature is to carry "sensation into the midst of the objects of the science itself," it must, as Dickens' novels do, describe the effect of the machine on the sensibility.

But if Kipling's machine literature fails to engage the changed emotional temper of the machine age, it does succeed more fully in extending the range of poetic language. He does not break completely with the nineteenth-century formulas for describing the machine; the personified ships and locomotives are logical extensions of earlier anthropomorphic descriptions of the machine. As Dickens describes steam engines as "melancholy, mad elephants," so Kipling sees a steam crane in similarly vitalistic terms: "An overhead crane travelled to and fro along its spile-pier, jerking sections of iron into place, snorting and backing and grunting as an elephant grunts in the timber-yard."[39] And yet Kipling's persistent vitalistic description, even in the extreme form of personification, is often not merely a facile use of convention but the expression of his own sense of the aliveness of inanimate objects, a perception allied to his mystical temperament. For example, he writes in a personal letter to Henley:

> The way collisions at sea come about is this . . . the iron in the mine and under the hammer, and in the plates and engine-room, has a sort of blind lust beaten into it, for to meet and I suppose nautically to copulate with other iron and steel being linked into the frame of another ship. All the seven seas over, the ship yearns for its mate, tearing along under moon and cloud . . . rust-

ing in dock; and so forth. At last comes the bridal night—wind, current and set of the sea aiding, while the eyes of men are held, and steamer meets steamer in a big kiss, and sink down to cool off in the water-beds.[40]

But if he could not escape completely from Victorian literary conventions, he did carry out his own revolutionary idea that technology should be described not in a language derived from romantic descriptions of nature, but in the very language of the technicians themselves. Kipling thus becomes the first writer to use the language of the engineer as the language of literature. This style is most effective when it expresses the clarity of the engineering mind in language denotative and unmetaphorical. As the analogue of the engineering plain style in architecture, this language is more suited to increasingly functionalist machinery and buildings than, for example, the richer style of Ruskin which so closely corresponds to the emotionally suggestive architecture it is used to celebrate. The opening description of Findlayson's bridge, "with its approaches, his work was one mile and three-quarters in length; a lattice-girder bridge, trussed with the Findlayson truss, standing on seven-and-twenty brick piers,"[41] although it reads like a specification for bids, is far more appropriate to its subject and to the scientific sensibility examined in the story than, for example, the vitalistic description of the steam crane as an elephant.

And yet the inherent problem in using technological language in poetry as well as in describing the inner life of the technologist in literature remains unsolved in Kipling. For it is not merely that the technical details of a turbine or a bridge cannot be fully understood by a nonscientist, but that it is exactly the knowledge that lies beyond the layman that is the source of beauty to the engineer. Quite simply, the delight of the engineer in a bridge or an engine depends upon an expertise and a language that is unintelligible to the average reader. The reader can only comprehend technology and the technologist if they are related to his own experience. The main reason for the success, and for the limitations, of Victorian writers on the machine is that, mystified by technology, they were forced to stay within the bounds of what they, and the layman, could understand. The locomotive is described as a dragon, the steam engine as an angry god; these conventional metaphors are then made to carry symbolic weight. When Kipling keeps his engineering idiom within these same bounds of common knowledge, as in the description of Findlayson's bridge, the prose succeeds in its simplicity and clarity. But when his work moves from journalism to arcana and the language from denotative prose to jargon, it becomes merely unintelligible. "McAndrew's Hymn" is, on the whole, successful because of restraint in the use of the engineering idiom which keeps the meaning at least vaguely intelligible. In a passage like "My seven thousand horse-power here. Eh, Lord! They're grand—they're grand!"[42] the technical language of the engineer becomes at least the comprehensible language of a dramatic monologue. But without a blueprint, a line like "An' now the main eccentrics start their quarrel on the sheaves"[43] can only be taken on faith, its effect depending less on meaning than on a purely rhythmic effect.

This transformation of scientific prose into a style that is made purposefully unintelligible so as to create a sense, not of the functional beauty of the machine, but of its mystery and power, is seen most clearly in "With the Night Mail." Here, Kipling invents fantastic machinery and equally fantastic language to describe it: "Here we find Fleury's Paradox of the Bulkheaded Vacuum—which we accept now without thought—literally in full blast. The three engines are H. T. & T. assisted-vacuo Fleury turbines running from 3000 to the Limit."[44] As this passage indicates, Kipling, dominated by his desire to be an insider, could not see that whereas technical language could create a style appropriate to the functional nature of the machine, used for its own sake such language could only make literature of the machine incomprehensible.

As his experiments in technological language testify, Kipling had absorbed the facts of mechanization far more fully than had most nineteenth-century writers. This imaginative grasp of the machine is shown, too, in his ability to use the machine in metaphors as vehicle rather than tenor. Before World War I, the machine served not only as an emblem of his social ideals but as a figure for psychological states unrelated to mechanization. When, at the end of the novel, Kim is torn between loyalty to the Lama and devotion to England, his mental state is objectified through a machine metaphor: "He felt, though he could not put it into words, that his soul was out of gear with its surroundings—a cog-wheel unconnected with any machinery, just like the idle cog-wheel of a cheap Behea sugar-crusher laid by in a corner."[45] In his final rejection of mysticism for the practical duties of British service, Kim is again compared to a machine: "With an almost audible click he felt the wheels of his being lock up anew on the world without."[46] Here, the machine figure does far more than describe the quality of mental life; through its symbolic associations it suggests approval of Kim's decision to subordinate himself to the state.

This use of the machine as a figure for ideas and emotions far removed from the facts of technological change is most effective in "McAndrew's Hymn." Here, the engineering idiom is the natural language of the speaker, the appropriate vehicle for his emotions. Within the context, there is nothing contrived in: "The sins o' four an' forty years, all up an' down the seas,/ Clack an' repeat like valves half-fed."[47] It is also conceivable that he might liken his religion to his engines. This comparison shows Kipling's almost metaphysical ability to link separate areas of knowledge, an ability that transcends the typical nineteenth-century dissociation of science and feeling:

> From coupler-flange to spindle-guide I see Thy
>   Hand, O God—
> Predestination in the stride o' yon connectin'-rod.
> John Calvin might ha' forged the same—
>   enorrmous, certain, slow—
> Ay, wrought it in the furnace-flame—*my*
>   "Institutio."[48]

But Kipling's use of the machine as metaphor, like

the romance of the machine, ultimately fails because it is based on untenable assumptions. The machine is just not the right figure for the shifting, flowing reality of psychic life. The figurative use of the machine can be effective as it is used in most nineteenth-century writing, to oppose the organic conception of the mind and of the state to the mechanistic; Morris' continual cry that the capitalist economy must be eradicated because it resembles a giant machine becomes effective polemic because both audience and author assume that the social system should not be regularized, impersonal, and repressive. But Kipling's rhetorical use of the machine metaphor rests on the assumption that the mind and the state should become more orderly, more disciplined, more rationalized. Kim can save his soul only by curbing his emotions, by connecting the wheel of his life to the machinery of the British Empire. "McAndrew's Hymn" succeeds as a Browningesque study and an experiment in metaphor; as a moral lesson extolling the discipline exemplified in a marine engine, it is somewhat less palatable. Only after the war, when Kipling examines the complexity of the human psyche, do his figures stress the dissimilarity between men and machines.

If Kipling's attempt to evoke the romance of the machine and expand the literary use of technological idiom was less than fully successful, his unexceptionable achievement was to broaden the subject matter of literature. For Kipling, the strange new machinery of the modern world became the subject of poetry as well as the source of metaphor. Furthermore, new inventions were incorporated into his stories almost as quickly as they appeared.[49] "Wireless" was written in the earliest days of radio work; "Mrs. Bathhurst" (1904) uses the newly invented cinema as the main plot device. And Kipling writes, too, of the technological skills, of the professional language, of the admiration for machinery that in the modern world go to make up the daily experience of many men. It is Kipling who carries "sensation" into the work of the engineer and the technologist, the ordinary men whose lives were enlivened, rather than degraded, by the technological revolution.

iii

After the horrors of World War I, after the death of his only son in France, Kipling changed. The vulgar patriot of Beerbohm's cartoon, "Mr. Rudyard Kipling takes a bloomin' day aht on the blasted 'eath, along with Britannia, 'is gurl," the small man dressed in checked suit with martial helmet and tiny trumpet became a writer deeply concerned with the regeneration of the shattered human mind. Having lost his faith in the psychological efficacy of duty and discipline, he came to value the spontaneous and intuitive. And in his writings the machine was returned to its typical nineteenth-century use as the symbol of the rationality and repression threatening the mind. The antitechnological impulses, subordinated in the prewar work, also became more explicit, moving his writing away from the romance of the machine toward the themes of earlier nineteenth-century literature.

Still, during his last years, Kipling continued to feel the romance of the machine. With his sensitivity to technological change, he saw that the airplane was replacing the P. & O. as the lifeline of the Empire and would replace the steamship as its emblem; by his desk, he notes in the last sentence of *Something of Myself,* stand "two big globes, on one of which a great airman had once outlined in white paint those air-routes to the East and Australia which were well in use before my death." The pilot became for Kipling the new embodiment of technologist as hero, and in exemplifying the primary virtues of courage and skill, the subject of a new epic literature. "Hymn of the Triumphant Airman, Flying East to West at 1000 M. P. H." (1929) continues the attempt to relate mechanized work to the traditional heroic modes, but the conventional language of the epic is quite inappropriate to the spare functionalism of its new subject:

> Oh, long had we paltered
> With bridle and girth
> Ere those horses were haltered
> That gave us the Earth—
>
> Ere the Flame and the Fountain,
> The Spark and the Wheel,
> Sank Ocean and Mountain
> Alike 'neath our keel . . .
>
> Till the gale was outdriven,
> The gull overflown,
> And there matched us in Heaven
> The Sun-God alone.[50]

After 1918 his transcendentalist criticism of mechanization becomes more explicit, both in the denigration of technological progress by comparison to a greater spiritual reality, a theme used equivocally in "The Bridge-Builders," and in the philosophical criticism of the machine as intellectual model for the natural world, as suggested earlier in "Wireless." "Unprofessional" (1930), for example, is a fictionalized attack on the mechanistic assumptions of science. In this tale, the protagonist, a wealthy astronomer and a serious believer in astrology, persuades some of his medical friends to correlate their biological research with his astrological observations. The physicians find that there are periodic "tides" running through the protoplasm under observation that seem to coincide with certain movements of the stars. By performing a difficult operation at a propitious astrological moment, the surgeons seem to succeed, only to find that they have to keep their patient from suicide when the great "tide" of the universe, flowing with the "tide" of her body, strains to sweep her to death. Kipling hardly believed in the specific biological theory he proposed, but he was serious in suggesting the limitations of a science based on the analogy of the universe as a machine: "We can't tell on what system this dam' dynamo of our universe is wound," says one of the scientists. "But we know we're in the middle of every sort of wave, as we call 'em. They used to be 'influences' . . . This rigid 'thinking' game is hanging up research."[51] The verse concluding the story is equally explicit in proposing an organic rather than a mechanistic model for nature:

They found one Breath in all things,
That blows all things between.
They proved one Matter in all things—
Eternal, changeless, unseen.[52]

Kipling became more explicit, too, in criticizing the tangible effects of technology. Whereas in his earlier writing doubts about mechanization were either equivocal, as in "The Bridge-Builders," or subordinated to a political theme, as in "As Easy as A.B.C.," in his later work the destructive results of mechanization became primary. In Kipling's usual manner, this social criticism is expressed indirectly, in a fable rather than in the realistic mode. "The Eye of Allah" (1926), his most explicit antimachine fable, is set in the Middle Ages. A monk recently returned from Spain demonstrates a primitive microscope, called "the eye of Allah" by the Moors, at a dinner given by his abbot. Although the guests, including Roger Bacon, are enthusiastic, the host commands that the instrument be destroyed. With the abbot's speech, Kipling opposes the nineteenth-century dream of a cohesive, preindustrial society represented by the Middle Ages to the destructiveness of mechanized war. Although there is still a touch of admiration for the machine, the abbot's speech would have pleased Ruskin and Morris:

> It would seem . . . the choice lies between two sins. To deny the world a Light which is under our hand, or to enlighten the world before her time. What you have seen, I saw long since among the physicians at Cairo . . . This birth, my sons, is untimely. It will be but the mother of more death, more torture, more division, and greater darkness in this dark age. Therefore I, who

know both my world and the Church, take this choice
on my conscience.[53]

He grinds the lenses beneath the hilt of his dagger.

No longer celebrated as the emblem of order and
progress, the machine still remains Kipling's central
symbol for the modern world. But, like Henry Adams,
Kipling now writes of technological power, represented
by the dynamo, as a malevolent force, barely held under
control. He says in "Song of the Dynamo" (1927):

> What do I care how you dispose
> The Powers that move me?
> I only know that I am one with those
> True Powers which rend the firmament above me,
> And, harrying earth, would save me at the last—
> But that your coward foresight holds me fast![54]

World War I, in which in the paradoxical fashion
of the twentieth century the increase in technological
skill only reduced war to a more savage, primitive business, had made Morris' vision of class warfare and even
Wells's prophecies of aerial warfare seem cozy day-
dreams. In his postwar stories, Kipling turns from cele-
brations of the machine itself to the effect of mechanization, in this case of mechanized warfare, on the mind.
And the terms he uses are those of the nineteenth
century, the opposition of healthy organic processes to
the unnatural repression both caused and symbolized by
the machine. This figurative contrast between the
machine-dominated external life and the spontaneous
inner life is seen most explicitly in "Woman in His
Life" (1928), a story from a late collection significantly

titled *Limits and Renewals* (1932). The protagonist, a veteran of the Great War, is a typical Kipling engineer, hard-working, successful in his machine-tool business. But here Kipling's former praise of the disciplined technician is inverted; for the first time, the psychological hazards of machine work intrude. An employee speaks to John, the engineer, about quitting:

> " 'Tain't a job—that's all. My machines do everything for me except strike. *I*'ve got to do that," said Jerry with reproach.
> "Soft job. Stick to it," John counselled.
> "Stick to bloomin' what? Turning two taps and fiddlin' three levers? Get a girl to do it for you. Repetition-work! I'm fed up!"
> "Take ten days' leave, you fool," said John.[55]

For the early Kipling, the call to emulate the discipline and rhythm of the machine would have been the highest wisdom; here the engineer's words are an ironic indication that the mind capable of designing machines is incapable of understanding the psyche. After this Gradgrind-like advice to his employee, John's own repressed emotions break out that night in nightmares reliving the experiences of the war:

> Being inarticulate, except where the Works were concerned, he explained that he felt as though he had got the hump—was stale, fed-up, and so forth. He thought, perhaps, he might have been working a bit too hard; but he said not a word of the horror, the blackness, the loss of the meaning of things, the collapses at the end, the recovery and retraversing of that night's Inferno; nor how it had waked up a certain secret dread which he had held off him since demobilisation.[56]

Only John's servant, whose feelings remain undistorted by scientific training, can suggest the needed therapy of emotional renewal. Here, the machine imagery is used to point to the value of flexibility and self-renewal in organic life: "Machinery suddenly arrested has no resources in itself. Human mechanism under strain finds comfort in a drink or two."[57] And if psychically destructive discipline and rationality are symbolized by the machine, healthy emotional life is represented here, as in *Hard Times,* by the intuitive wisdom of animals. A trained horse and dog become the agents of charity rather than calculation in allowing Tom Gradgrind to escape; Merrylegs finds his way back to the horse riders. In Kipling's story the engineer is saved by a dog. The servant buys John a dog, and the tale lapses into sentimentality as John discovers his emotions in growing to love the animal. But given the simplistic emotion of the tale, the point is clear, and the moral is the consistent theme of Victorian literature— in the intuitive self lies the only safeguard of the psyche in a mechanized world.

With his late stories and poems of the machine, Kipling returns to the dominant attitudes of earlier Victorian literature. In his last poems, the images drawn from the twentieth-century technology of concrete and steel suggest, not romance, but the limitations of rationalized science:

> The prudent text-books give it
> In tables at the end—
> The stress that shears a rivet
> Or makes a tie-bar bend—

What traffic wrecks macadam—
What concrete should endure—
But we, poor Sons of Adam,
Have no such literature,
To warn us or make sure! ...

Oh, veiled and secret Power
Whose paths we seek in vain,
Be with us in our hour
Of overthrow and pain;
That we—by which sure token
We know Thy ways are true—
In spite of being broken,
Because of being broken,
May rise and build anew.
Stand up and build anew.[58]

Conclusion

It was not until the end of the century, then, that the machine came to be considered a subject as worthy of poetic treatment as a rose, a Renaissance bishop, or romantic love. The continuance of the romantic belief that art must be intuitive as well as expressive prevented the Victorians from recognizing in the machine a new form of beauty whose defining quality is regularity and the logical fitting of form to function. And without a viable aesthetic of the machine, the Victorian writer turned to literary forms that evade confronting the machine as aesthetic object. The literary habit of using the machine as tenor rather than vehicle, the innumerable comparisons of locomotives to horses and dragons, exemplifies this inability to see the machine as a visible object with its own unique aesthetic qualities. Even the technological sublime does not describe the machine itself but only uses it as a stimulus to create a delightful shudder. Carlyle thrilling to the awakening of Manchester, Dickens concentrating on the grotesquerie of the railway yards, Ruskin warning of the steam engine as a diabolic manifestation, all indicate Victorian authors' occupation with their emotional response to the machine rather than with the machine itself. Even in Wells's evolutionary fantasies, the machine is not described with detailed precision but used primarily as a vaguely defined background suggesting the menacing quality of mechanized life.

This forcing of the machine into traditional, and often inappropriate, literary conventions—the sublime, personification, the pastoral—is but one example of the deep-seated confusion about the aesthetic value of the machine that runs through all the Victorian arts. The Doric capitals on stamping presses, the electroplated silver spaniels reclining on the table silver, the Doric Propylaea guarding the entrance to Euston station, all indicate in their application of traditional artistic conventions to new machine forms and processes the same failure to recognize, and to value the aesthetic qualities of the machine. And just as in opposition to the Gothic revival some architects and engineers were instinctively grasping the aesthetic possibilities of machine-made objects, so too some Victorian writers were violating literary convention in order to make the machine a respectable literary subject and to develop a literary language derived from the new technology. In their attempt to realize the particular beauty of the machine and to break down the limiting nineteenth-century antithesis between intellect and emotion, between science and art, the work of Wells and Kipling, and to a lesser extent of Henley and Davidson, is the literary analogue of contemporaneous developments in design, of Voysey's furniture and Mackintosh's functional buildings. This is not to posit a teleology in which literature fulfills its true nature as it comes to include the machine, but only to suggest that the idea of Victorian literature as bent solely on offering emotional solace to machine-age man is incomplete in missing the antithetical desire of writers to find in the mechanized world new sources of emotional strength as well as of beauty. And if at first the mechanized world seemed only a slum into which the polite writer ventured either for mild excitement or to gather material for a reforming tract, gradually many came to feel that this machine-made world had its own particular beauties, some indeed far more striking than the floral decoration and mythological friezes on the Palace of Art.

Of the varying Victorian modes for treating the machine in the absence of a machine aesthetic, the most effective, and the most common, is the symbolic, for it enables the writer to subordinate the aesthetic question to the moral purposes of his writing. Within the transcendental assumptions of much early Victorian writing, the machine, like any phenomenon, is important not as a visible fact but as the manifestation of an inward spiritual principle. The early Victorian writers on the machine thus speak as prophets rather than as aestheticians. For Carlyle the machine is a *sign* of the times, like the hero a tangible manifestation of the providential forces shaping England. Similarly, for all Ruskin's concern with the aesthetic implications of mechanization, machine art is still most significant as an emblem of the moral qualities of his age. His writing moves inevitably from aesthetic to social criticism of the machine age until, in his later work, the machine appears as an apocalyptic symbol of an evil principle informing the visible world.

Throughout the century, the machine as symbol serves not only as a convenient figure for the complex forces shaping the age but becomes an implicit measure of value as well. Nothing is more striking in the Victorian literary response to technology than the consistently pejorative sense attached to the word "machine" and its derivatives once they are taken beyond a strictly denotative use. This critical tone is not directed at technological progress per se. Toward the machine itself, all writers were ambivalent, generally feeling a kind of fearful awe. Rather, the force of the antimachine feeling in Victorian literature is directed at the machine as a manifestation of and symbol for what may best be called the scientific habit of mind, the desire to reduce the complex operations of the natural world, of society, and of the psyche to a few simple, quantitative laws.

This consistency underlying the varied uses of the machine as symbol suggests a major continuity in Victorian literature in its attack on rationalizing, abstracting modes of thought. Dickens' satire of political economy in *Hard Times* and Morris' rejection of Bellamy's industrial armies in *News from Nowhere* both criticize the attempt to regulate social activity by abstract law. Similarly, Carlyle's rejection of the mechan-

istic hypothesis in philosophy and Butler's opposition
to the man-machine analogy in biology are both re-
actions against the explanation of natural phenomena
by the scientific method. And so, too, Ruskin's assumption that the engineer, working by rule and line, could
never comprehend the moral energy manifested in the
visible world continues in more secular form in Wells's
scientific romances dramatizing the necessary amorality
of the scientific intellect.

Throughout Victorian writing, the machine as
symbol for the scientific mind is opposed to another set
of metaphors that might generally be termed "organic."
The emphasis on organicism links the transcendentalism of Carlyle's "natural supernaturalism," the ideal
of organic form that Ruskin opposes to the rationalistic order of machine art, and the vitalism Butler pro-
poses to replace mechanistic biological theory. The
term "organic" suggests, too, the ideal of the organic
society, the disappearing feudal matrix of loyalty and
obligation that was so consistently attractive to the
Victorians. And yet the simple organic-mechanistic
antithesis does not indicate the deeply intuitionist
assumptions that lie behind the literary opposition to
the modes of thought and social organization represented by the machine. Here the influence of Carlyle,
as the prophet of the Coleridgean tradition, is central,
as important to Dickens' assumption of an instinctive
moral sense corrupted by utilitarian society as to
Ruskin's belief in an equally instinctive creative ability
degraded by mechanized production.

From this intuitionism, and in reaction to the

combination of industrialism, scientific thought, and emotional discipline symbolized by the machine, there developed in Victorian literature an increasingly stronger strain of primitivism. Abbot Samson and his monks, drowning self-consciousness in rough work, Ruskin's untutored medieval stonecarver expressing his simple reverence in crude religious sculpture, are the main actors in the Victorian drama of historical decline. Dickens' horseriders remain both creative and moral by resisting a scientific education and regularized work. This Victorian primitivism culminates in *News from Nowhere,* the most radical Victorian critique of mechanized life, in which not only machine work, but any belief in work as a value in itself, is rejected in favor of a life in which the spontaneous release of vital, strongly sexual energy becomes the chief good.

In the machine, then, the Victorian literary imagination saw incarnated the power of the scientific intellect, and the finest writing on the machine centers upon the alliance of this abstracting intellect with the immense physical and social power of technology itself. The opposition to mechanized production, the celebration of hand labor, the aesthetic distaste for the machine are but expressions of the deeper conflict between rationalism and intuitionism, between scientific and organic modes of thought that is the true subject of the Victorian writing on the machine.

Selected Bibliography

Notes

Index

Selected Bibliography

Samuel Butler

Amis, Kingsley. "Afterword," *Erewhon*. New York, 1961.

Butler, Samuel. *The Collected Works of Samuel Butler*, ed. Henry Festing Jones and A. T. Bartholomew. 20 vols. London, 1923-1926.

—— *Erewhon*. London, 1872.

—— *Samuel Butler's Notebooks*, ed. Geoffrey Keynes and Brian Hill. New York, 1951.

Furbank, P. N. *Samuel Butler*. Cambridge, Eng., 1948.

Joad, C. E. M. *Samuel Butler*. London, 1924.

Jones, Henry Festing. *Samuel Butler, Author of Erewhon: A Memoir*. 2 vols. London, 1919.

Knoepflmacher, Ulrich. *Religious Humanism and the Victorian Novel*. Princeton, 1965.

Muggeridge, Malcolm. *The Earnest Atheist*. London, 1936.

Willey, Basil. *Darwin and Butler, Two Versions of Evolution*. London, 1960.

Wilson, Edmund. "The Satire of Samuel Butler," *The Triple Thinkers*. New York, 1938, pp. 210-219.

Thomas Carlyle

Carlyle, Thomas. *The Works of Thomas Carlyle.* 30 vols. London, 1896-1899.

―――― *Last Words of Thomas Carlyle, On Trades-Unions, Promoterism and the Signs of the Times.* Edinburgh, 1882.

―――― *Reminiscences,* ed. James Anthony Froude. New York, 1881.

DeLaura, David J. "Arnold and Carlyle," *PMLA,* 79:103-129 (1964).

Froude, James Anthony. *Thomas Carlyle: A History of His Life in London.* 2 vols. New York, 1884.

―――― *Thomas Carlyle: A History of the First Forty Years of His Life.* 2 vols. New York, 1882.

Harrold, Charles F. "The Nature of Carlyle's Calvinism," *Studies in Philology,* 33:475-486 (July 1936).

Murphy, Ella M. "Carlyle and the Saint Simonians," *Studies in Philology,* 33:93-118 (January 1936).

Neff, Emery. *Carlyle.* New York, 1932.

―――― *Carlyle and Mill.* New York, 1926.

Shine, Hill, *Carlyle and the Saint Simonians: The Concept of Historical Periodicity.* Baltimore, 1941.

Charles Dickens

Dickens, Charles. *American Notes.* New York, 1893.

―――― *Dombey and Son.* New York, 1892.

―――― "The Flight," *Household Words,* 3:529-533 (August 30, 1851).

―――― *Hard Times.* New York, 1895.

―――― *The Lazy Tour of Two Idle Apprentices.* New York, 1896.

―――― *The Letters of Charles Dickens,* ed. Walter Dexter. 3 vols. Bloomsbury: Nonesuch Press, 1938.

―――― "Mugby Junction," *Christmas Stories.* New York, 1896.

―――― *The Old Curiosity Shop.* New York, 1897.

―――― *Our Mutual Friend.* New York, 1895.

―――― *Pickwick Papers.* New York, 1897.

———— "A Poor Man's Tale of a Patent," *Household Words,* 2: 73-75 (October 19, 1850).

———— *Sketches by Boz.* New York, 1892.

———— *The Speeches of Charles Dickens,* ed. K. J. Fielding. Oxford, 1960.

———— *The Uncommercial Traveller.* New York, 1896.

Gissing, George. *Charles Dickens: A Critical Study.* New York, 1904.

House, Humphrey. *The Dickens World.* London, 1960.

Johnson, Edgar. *Charles Dickens: His Tragedy and Triumph.* 2 vols. New York, 1952.

Leavis, F. R. *The Great Tradition.* London, 1950.

Orwell, George. "Charles Dickens," *A Collection of Essays.* Garden City, 1954, pp. 55-110.

Wilson, Edmund. "Dickens: The Two Scrooges," *The Wound and the Bow.* New York, 1941, pp. 1-104.

Rudyard Kipling

Annan, Noel. "Kipling's Place in the History of Ideas," *Victorian Studies,* 3:323-348 (June 1960).

Carrington, C. E. *The Life of Rudyard Kipling.* New York, 1955.

Eliot, T. S. *A Choice of Kipling's Verse.* London, 1941.

Kipling, Rudyard. *The Sussex Edition of the Complete Works in Prose and Verse of Rudyard Kipling.* 35 vols. London, 1937-1939.

———— *Rudyard Kipling's Verse, Definitive Edition.* New York, 1940.

Orwell, George. "Rudyard Kipling," *A Collection of Essays.* Garden City, 1954, pp. 123-138.

Tompkins, J. M. S. *The Art of Rudyard Kipling.* London, 1959.

Trilling, Lionel. "Kipling," *The Liberal Imagination.* Garden City, 1957, pp. 114-124.

Wilson, Edmund. "The Kipling That Nobody Read," *The Wound and the Bow.* New York, 1941, pp. 105-181.

William Morris

Burne-Jones, Edward. "MS. Account Books of Work with Morris and Company." Fitzwilliam Museum, Cambridge, England.

Burne-Jones, Georgiana. *Memorials of Edward Burne-Jones.* 2 vols. New York, 1906.

Crow, Gerald H. *William Morris: Designer.* London, 1934.

Floud, Peter. "William Morris as an Artist," *Listener,* 53:562-564, 615-617 (October 7 and 14, 1954).

Mackail, J. W. *The Life of William Morris.* 2 vols. London, 1899.

Morris, Barbara. "William Morris, A Twentieth Century View of his Woven Textiles," *Handweaver & Craftsman,* 12:6-11, 54-55 (Spring 1961).

Morris, May. *William Morris: Artist, Writer, Socialist.* 2 vols. Oxford, 1936.

Morris, William. *Letters of William Morris to His Family and Friends,* ed. Philip Henderson. London, 1950.

———— "Typescript of Letters of William Morris to Sir Thomas Wardle." Victoria and Albert Museum, MS. Box II.86.ZZ.

———— *Works of William Morris,* ed. May Morris. 24 vols. London, 1910-1915.

Taylor, George Warrington. "MS. Letters." Victoria and Albert Museum, MS.RC.HH. 4.

Tillotson, Geoffrey. "Morris and the Machine," *Fortnightly Review,* 141:464-471 (April 1934).

Vallance, Aymer. *William Morris: His Art, His Writings and His Public Life.* London, 1897.

Webb, Philip. "Account Books of Work with Morris and Company." MS. in the possession of Mr. Brandon-Jones of Hampstead, England.

John Ruskin

Clark, Kenneth. *John Ruskin.* Oxford, 1947.

Quennell, Peter. *John Ruskin.* New York, 1949.

Ruskin, John. *The Works of John Ruskin,* ed. E. T. Cook and Alexander Wedderburn. 39 vols. London, 1903-1912.

Rosenberg, John D. *The Darkening Glass.* New York, 1961.
Wilenski, Reginald H. *John Ruskin.* London, 1933.

H. G. Wells

Amis, Kingsley. *New Maps of Hell.* New York, 1960.
Bergonzi, Bernard. *The Early H. G. Wells: A Study of the Scientific Romances.* Manchester, 1961.
Pritchett, V. S. "The Scientific Romances," *The Living Novel.* London, 1946, pp. 116-124.
Ray, Gordan N. "H. G. Wells Tries to Be a Novelist," *Edwardians and Late Victorians* (English Institute Essays, 1959). New York, 1960.
Wagar, W. Warren. *H. G. Wells and the World State.* New Haven, 1961.
Wells, Geoffry H. *H. G. Wells: A Bibliography, Dictionary and Subject-Index.* London, 1926.
Wells, H. G. *Anticipations.* New York, 1902.
—— *Certain Personal Matters.* London, 1901.
—— *The Discovery of the Future.* London, 1902.
—— *Experiment in Autobiography.* 2 vols. London, 1934.
—— *The Food of the Gods,* in *Seven Famous Novels by H. G. Wells.* New York, 1934.
—— *The Invisible Man,* in *Seven Famous Novels by H. G. Wells.* New York, 1934.
—— *The Island of Dr. Moreau,* in *Seven Famous Novels by H. G. Wells.* New York, 1934.
—— *Mind at the End of Its Tether.* London, 1945.
—— *The First Men in the Moon,* in *Seven Famous Novels by H. G. Wells.* New York, 1934.
—— *A Modern Utopia.* London, 1905.
—— *The Short Stories of H. G. Wells.* London, 1927.
—— *The War of the Worlds,* in *Seven Famous Novels by H. G. Wells.* New York, 1934.
—— *When the Sleeper Wakes.* New York, 1899.
West, Anthony. "H. G. Wells," *Encounter,* 8:52-59 (February 1957).

Other Works

Abrams, M. H. *The Mirror and the Lamp*. New York, 1953.

Arnold, Matthew. *Culture and Anarchy*, ed. Dover Wilson. Cambridge, Eng., 1960.

Ashton, T. S. *The Industrial Revolution*. London, 1955.

Briggs, Asa. *1851*. London, 1951.

Buckley, Jerome H. *The Victorian Temper*. Cambridge, Mass., 1951.

Coleridge, S. T. *Biographia Literaria*, ed. J. Shawcross. 2 vols. Oxford, 1907.

Davidson, John. *Fleet Street and Other Poems*. London, 1909.

Derry, T. K. and Trevor I. Williams. *A Short History of Technology*. New York, 1961.

Disraeli, Benjamin. *Coningsby*. London, 1881.

—— *Sybil; or The Two Nations*. London, 1845.

Dubos, Rene. *The Dreams of Reason*. New York, 1961.

Ellul, Jacques. *Technological Society*. New York, 1965.

Fisher, Marvin. "The Iconology of Industrialism, 1830-60," *American Quarterly*, 13:347-364 (Fall 1961).

Gaskell, Elizabeth. *Mary Barton*. Oxford, 1906.

—— *North and South*. London, 1906.

Giedion, Sigfried. *Mechanization Takes Command*. New York, 1948.

—— *Space, Time and Architecture*. Cambridge, Mass., 1949.

Ginestier, Paul. *The Poet and the Machine*, trans. Martin B. Friedman. Chapel Hill, 1961.

Halévy, Élie. *A History of the English People in 1815*. New York, 1924.

Henley, W. E. *Poems*. London, 1921.

Hough, Graham. *The Last Romantics*. London, 1949.

Huxley, T. H. "On the Hypothesis That Animals are Automata," *Method and Results*. New York, 1896.

Klingender, Francis. *Art and the Industrial Revolution*. London, 1947.

McLuhan, Marshall. *Understanding Media*. New York, 1965.

Marcuse, Herbert. *Eros and Civilization*. Boston, 1955.

Marx, Leo. *The Machine in the Garden.* New York, 1965.

—— "Two Kingdoms of Force," *Massachusetts Review,* 1: 72-95 (October 1959).

Measom, George. *Official Illustrated Guide to the London and North-Western Railway.* London, 1856.

Mill, John Stuart. *On Liberty.*

—— "Tocqueville on Democracy in America," *Essays on Politics and Culture.* Garden City, 1963.

Mumford, Lewis. *Art and Technics.* New York, 1960.

—— *Technics and Civilization.* New York, 1934.

Pevsner, Nikolaus. *High Victorian Design.* London, 1951.

—— *Pioneers of Modern Design.* New York, 1949.

Read, Herbert. *Art and Industry.* Bloomington, Indiana, 1961.

Riesman, David. *The Lonely Crowd.* Garden City, 1953.

Singer, C., E. J. Holmyard, A. R. Hall, eds. *A History of Technology.* 5 vols. Oxford, 1954-1958.

Smiles, Samuel. *The Life of George Stephenson.* London, 1868.

Trilling, Lionel. *The Liberal Imagination.* Garden City, 1957.

Ure, Andrew. *The Philosophy of Manufactures.* London, 1835.

Usher, Abbott Payson. *A History of Mechanical Inventions.* Boston, 1959.

Warburg, Jeremy. "Poetry and Industrialism," *Modern Language Review,* 53:161-170 (April 1958).

—— ed. *The Industrial Muse.* London, 1958.

Weber, Max. *The Protestant Ethic and the Spirit of Capitalism,* trans. Talcott Parsons. New York, 1950.

Whitehead, Alfred North. *Science and the Modern World.* New York, 1926.

Williams, Frederick. *Our Iron Roads.* London, 1852.

Williams, Raymond. *Culture and Society, 1780-1950.* Garden City, 1960.

Wordsworth, William. *The Poetical Works of Wordsworth.* London, 1950.

Young, G. M., ed. *Early Victorian England.* 2 vols. London, 1934.

Notes

Introduction

1. Samuel Smiles, *The Life of George Stephenson* (London, 1868), p. 262.

2. See the Victorian selections in the excellent collection of poetry of the machine edited by Jeremy Warburg, *The Industrial Muse* (London, 1958).

3. "Prologue" to *The Earthly Paradise,* in *Works of William Morris,* ed. May Morris (London, 1910-1915), III, 3.

4. *Essays on Politics and Culture,* ed. Gertrude Himmelfarb (New York, 1962), p. 262.

5. The most important statement of this theory is Alfred North Whitehead, *Science and the Modern World* (New York, 1925), chap. v.

6. *Three Essays by John Stuart Mill* (London, 1912), p. 73.

7. "Signs of the Times," *The Works of Thomas Carlyle* (London, 1896-1899), XXVII, 59.

8. "Reality in America," *The Liberal Imagination* (Garden City, 1957), p. 7.

9. The two styles in architecture are discussed by Sigfried Giedion, *Space, Time and Architecture* (Cambridge, Mass., 1949).

10. Preface to *Milton.*

11. Bk. VIII, ll. 164-169.

12. *The Excursion,* Bk. VIII, ll. 287-291.

13. *Technics and Civilization* (New York, 1934), chap. iv.

14. *Ibid.,* chap. v.

15. *Culture and Anarchy,* ed. J. Dover Wilson (Cambridge, Eng., 1961), p. 50.

Chapter I: Thomas Carlyle

1. *Works of Thomas Carlyle* (London, 1896-1899), XXVII, 80-81. All subsequent citations of volume and page number refer to this edition.

2. I, 179.

3. I, 183.

4. James Anthony Froude, *Thomas Carlyle: A History of the First Forty Years of His Life* (New York, 1882), I, 187.

5. Hill Shine, *Carlyle and the Saint Simonians: The Concept of Historical Periodicity* (Baltimore, 1941), chap. i.

6. XXVII, 59.

7. XXVII, 59.

8. Arnold's debt to Carlyle in this, and other matters, is explored fully in David J. DeLaura, "Arnold and Carlyle," *PMLA*, 79:104-129 (1964).

9. "Signs of the Times," XXVII, 66.

10. XXVII, 71.

11. See Francis Klingender, *Art and the Industrial Revolution* (London, 1947), pp. 58-86.

12. "Signs of the Times," XXVII, 61.

13. XXVII, 60.

14. XXVII, 61-62.

15. XXVII, 69-70.

16. XXVII, 61.

17. XXVII, 61.

18. XXVII, 61.

19. XXVII, 66.

20. XXVII, 66.

21. XXVII, 66.

22. XXVII, 71.

23. XXVII, 72.

24. XXVII, 63.

25. XXVII, 64.

26. XXVII, 60.

27. XXVII, 59-60.

28. XXVII, 73.

29. James Anthony Froude, *Thomas Carlyle: A History of His Life in London* (New York, 1884), I, 144.

30. *Past and Present*, X, 159.

31. "Chartism," XXIX, 181.

32. *Past and Present*, X, 276.

33. "Chartism," XXIX, 182.

34. "Corn-Law Rhymes," XXVIII, 138.

35. "Chartism," XXIX, 183.
36. *Sartor Resartus,* I, 133.
37. "Chartism," XXIX, 181.
38. "Chartism," XXIX, 181.
39. This discussion of painting is deeply indebted to Klingender (see n. 11 above), especially chap. iii.
40. See Wordsworth's "On the Projected Kendal and Windermere Railway" and the *Excursion,* Bk. VIII.
41. Klingender, *Art and the Industrial Revolution,* p. 177.
42. XXVIII, 156.
43. Klingender, *Art and the Industrial Revolution,* Plate III, pp. 16-17.
44. *Past and Present,* X, 228.
45. "Chartism," XXIX, 182.
46. "Chartism," XXIX, 181.
47. "Chartism," XXIX, 184.
48. *Past and Present,* X, 66.
49. "Chartism," XXIX, 171.
50. "Chartism," XXIX, 135.
51. "Chartism," XXIX, 141.
52. "Chartism," XXIX, 143.
53. "Chartism," XXIX, 143.
54. *Past and Present,* X, 212.
55. XXX, 32.
56. In this connection, it is interesting to note that Lewis Mumford in *Technics and Civilization* suggests that the medieval monastery, with its regulation of duties by the artifical time of the clock, is the first mechanized social institution. Carlyle's choice of a monastery as the emblem of an ideal factory is, then, quite apt.
57. *Past and Present,* X, 249.
58. X, 273.
59. XX, 256.
60. *Past and Present,* X, 274.

Chapter II: Charles Dickens

1. Judging the response to machine technology by the use of the machine as vehicle rather than tenor is suggested by Jeremy Warburg, "Poetry and Industrialism," *Modern Language Review,* 53:161-170 (April 1958).
2. See G. M. Young (ed.), *Early Victorian England* (London, 1934), I, 25-30.

3. *The Speeches of Charles Dickens,* ed. K. J. Fielding (Oxford, 1960), p. 62.

4. "The Flight," in *Household Words,* 3:532-533 (August 30, 1851).

5. *Coningsby* (London, 1881), p. 154.

6. London, 1906, pp. 92-93.

7. *Letters of Charles Dickens,* ed. Walter Dexter (Bloomsbury: Nonesuch Press, 1938), II, 338-339.

8. From a list in Edgar Johnson, *Charles Dickens: His Tragedy and Triumph* (New York, 1952), II, 708.

9. Dexter, *Letters,* II, 523.

10. George Gissing, *Charles Dickens: A Critical Study* (New York, 1904), p. 42.

11. Quoted in Fielding, *Speeches,* p. 62, n. 1.

12. "Mugby Junction," *Christmas Stories* (New York, 1896), pp. 464-465.

13. "Chatham Dockyard," *The Uncommercial Traveller* (New York, 1896), p. 228.

14. New York, 1892, p. 93.

15. Page 95.

16. New York, 1895, p. 422.

17. New York, 1897, p. 671.

18. New York, 1897, p. 309.

19. *Coningsby,* p. 153.

20. *Mary Barton* (Oxford, 1906), p. 261.

21. Francis Klingender, *Art and the Industrial Revolution* (London, 1947), pp. 103-114.

22. Page 316.

23. New York, 1892, p. 60.

24. New York, 1896, p. 372.

25. Page 458.

26. *Household Words,* 2:73 (October 19, 1850).

27. Page 263.

28. Page 174.

29. Page 37.

30. Page 263.

31. Page 264.

32. Page 695.

33. Page 725.

34. *Coningsby,* Bk. IV, chaps. i-ii.

35. *Dombey,* p. 205.

36. Page 206.

37. Page 17.

38. Page 499.

39. Page 499.

40. New York, 1895, p. 434.

41. *American Notes* (New York, 1893), chaps. liii-lxi.
42. Page 437.
43. Page 500.
44. Page 437.
45. Page 475.
46. Page 509.
47. *Works of Thomas Carlyle* (London, 1896-1899), XXVII, 61.
48. *Hard Times,* p. 426.
49. Page 422.
50. Dexter, *Letters,* II, 567.
51. *Hard Times,* p. 500.
52. Page 475.
53. Pages 541-542.
54. Page 618.
55. Page 471.
56. Pages 488-489.
57. Page 489.
58. Fielding, *Speeches,* p. 61.
59. *Ibid.,* p. 81.
60. *The Old Curiosity Shop,* p. 219.
61. Fielding, *Speeches,* p. 284.
62. *The Philosophy of Manufactures* (London, 1835), p. 15.
63. *North and South,* pp. 498-499.
64. Fielding, *Speeches,* p. 63.
65. Humphrey House, in *The Dickens World* (London, 1960), p. 220, points to this contradiction in Dickens' novels.
66. Page 309.
67. Page 499.
68. Page 465.
69. Page 458.
70. Page 311.
71. Johnson, *Charles Dickens,* II, 797.

Chapter III: John Ruskin

1. This notion of anonymous style is discussed in detail by Sigfried Giedion, *Space, Time and Architecture* (Cambridge, Mass., 1949).
2. *Works of John Ruskin,* ed. E. T. Cook and Alexander Wedderburn (Library Edition, London, 1903-1912), *Praeterita,* XXXV, 315. All subsequent citations of volume and page number refer to this edition.
3. Preface to *The Two Paths,* XVI, 251.
4. *Modern Painters I,* III, 542.

5. *Ibid.,* p. 563.
6. *Modern Painters II,* IV, 88.
7. *Seven Lamps of Architecture,* VIII, 66.
8. *Modern Painters III,* V, 155.
9. *Modern Painters IV,* VI, 333.
10. *Seven Lamps,* VIII, 219.
11. *The Two Paths,* XVI, 394-395.
12. *Ibid.,* p. 295.
13. *Modern Painters II,* IV, 284.
14. *Deucalion,* XXVI, 338.
15. The discussion of the romantic aesthetic is based upon Meyer Abrams, *The Mirror and the Lamp* (New York, 1953), especially chap. xi.
16. Giedion, *Space, Time and Architecture,* p. 116.
17. "On the Opening of the Crystal Palace," XII, 419-420.
18. *Stones of Venice,* IX, 67.
19. *Sesame and Lilies,* XVIII, 167.
20. *Stones of Venice,* X, 184.
21. X, 189.
22. X, 197.
23. X, 197.
24. X, 193.
25. XVII, 25.
26. XVII, 26.
27. XVII, 29.
28. XVII, 29-30.
29. XVII, 105.
30. XVII, 94-95.
31. "White Thorn Blossom," *Fors Clavigera,* XXVII, 79-97.
32. Because of his father's objections, Ruskin delayed publishing the ideas of *Unto This Last.*
33. XVII, 31.
34. IV, 47.
35. IV, 47.
36. *The Two Paths,* XVI, 339.
37. XVI, 339.
38. XVI, 340-341.
39. XXXIV, 267-268.
40. *Modern Painters III,* V, 380-381.
41. *Friendship's Garland,* in *The Complete Prose Works of Matthew Arnold,* ed. R. H. Super (Ann Arbor, Michigan, 1965), V, 21-22.
42. *Fors,* XXVII, 85. Cf. Thoreau in *Walden,* chap. i: "We are in great haste to construct a magnetic telegraph from Maine to Texas; but Maine and Texas, it may be, have nothing important to communicate."

43. The discussion here is close to Raymond Williams' analysis in *Culture and Society*. But as the comparison of Ruskin and Arnold illustrates, Professor Williams fails to emphasize the primitivistic strain in the nineteenth-century response to industrialism.

44. XXVIII, 206.

45. *Praeterita*, XXXV, 428.

46. *Fors*, XXVIII, 419.

47. XXVIII, 248.

48. *General Statement Explaining the Nature and Purposes of St. George's Guild*, XXX, 48.

49. *Munera Pulveris*, XVII, 156.

50. *Fors*, XXVIII, 655.

51. *St. George's Guild*, XXX, 48.

52. *Lectures on Art*, XX, 113-114. See also *Fors*, XXVIII, 138.

53. *St. George's Guild*, XXX, 48.

54. See John D. Rosenberg, *The Darkening Glass* (New York, 1961), pp. 71-78, for an interesting discussion of Ruskin's influence on Frank Lloyd Wright.

55. *The Crown of Wild Olive*, XVIII, 513.

56. *Munera Pulveris*, XVII, 273.

57. *Modern Painters III*, V, 380.

58. "The most horrible serpent dream I ever had yet in my life. The deadliest came out into the room under a door. It rose up like a cobra—with horrible round eyes and had woman's, or at least Medusa's breasts . . . another small one fastened on my neck and nothing would pull it off." Quoted in Rosenberg, *The Darkening Glass*, p. 169, n. 12.

59. XXIX, 548.

60. XXVII, 267.

61. *The Cestus of Aglaia*, XIX, 60-61.

62. XIX, 61.

63. Rosenberg, *The Darkening Glass*, pp. 213-214.

64. XXXIV, 40.

65. XXVII, 91.

66. XXVII, 92.

67. XXVII, 256.

Chapter IV: William Morris

1. May Morris, *William Morris: Artist, Writer, Socialist* (Oxford, 1936), II, 16.

2. J. W. Mackail, *The Life of William Morris* (London, 1899), I, 47.

3. May Morris, *WM: Artist, Writer, Socialist,* II, 9.

4. *Ibid.,* I, 292.

5. Morris gave his first public lecture on art in 1877, at the age of forty-three.

6. "The Beauty of Life," *Works of William Morris,* ed. May Morris (London, 1910-1915), XXII, 53. All subsequent citations of volume and page number refer to this edition, unless otherwise indicated.

7. "The Lesser Arts," XXII, 18.

8. XXII, 42.

9. "How We Live and How We might Live," XXIII, 8-9.

10. See Barbara Morris, "William Morris," *Handweaver and Craftsman,* 12:6-11, 54-55 (Spring 1961).

11. "Architecture and History," XXII, 311.

12. "Technical Instruction," in May Morris, *WM: Artist, Writer, Socialist,* I, 209-210.

13. "The Art of the People," XXII, 43.

14. "The Prospects of Architecture in Civilization," XXII, 143.

15. See Peter Floud, "William Morris as an Artist," *Listener,* 52:562-564, 615-617 (October 7 and 14, 1954), and Barbara Morris, "William Morris," *Handweaver and Craftsman* (Spring 1961).

16. George Warrington Taylor to Philip Webb, Victoria and Albert Museum, MS. RC. HH. 4., Letter 47.

17. Philip Webb's account books are in the possession of Mr. Brandon-Jones of Hampstead, England. The Burne-Jones Papers are in the Fitzwilliam Museum, Cambridge, England.

18. Aymer Vallance, *William Morris: His Art, His Writings and His Public Life* (London, 1897), pp. 121-122.

19. *Ibid.,* p. 72.

20. "Typescript of Letters of William Morris to Sir Thomas Wardle," Victoria and Albert Museum, MS. Box II. 86. ZZ, Letter 3.

21. "Letters to Wardle," Letter 9, November 5, 1875.

22. Mackail, *Life of William Morris,* II, 58.

23. "Letters to Wardle," Letter 49, April 13, 1877.

24. "Some Hints on Pattern-Designing," XXII, 204.

25. "Textiles," in May Morris, *WM: Artist, Writer, Socialist,* I, 245.

26. "The Lesser Arts of Life," XXII, 249-250.

27. Floud, "William Morris as an Artist," p. 616.

28. "Letters to Wardle," Letter 12, November 23, 1875.

29. "Making the Best of It," XXII, 112.

30. "The Beauty of Life," XXII, 76.

31. "The Art of the People," XXII, 48.

32. See Floud, "William Morris as an Artist," p. 564, for a more detailed discussion of this point.

33. "Art and the Beauty of the Earth," XXII, 169.

34. "Art and Its Producers," XXII, 352.

35. XXIII, 11.

36. XXIII, 11-12.

37. III, 3.

38. XXIV, 405.

39. "War," *The Crown of Wild Olive,* in *Works of John Ruskin,* ed. E. T. Cook and Alexander Wedderburn (London, 1903-1919), XVIII, 459-493.

40. "Art, Wealth, and Riches," XXIII, 160.

41. "The Revival of Architecture," XXII, 323.

42. XVI, xxviii.

43. *Works of Thomas Carlyle* (London, 1896-1899), X, 1.

44. "Art and Industry in the Fourteenth Century," XXII, 389.

45. XVI, 179.

46. Lines 167-170.

47. Lines 165-166.

48. *News from Nowhere,* XVI, 132.

49. XVI, 96.

50. "Art, Wealth, and Riches," XXIII, 160.

51. *News from Nowhere,* XVI, 97.

52. XVI, 162.

53. Boston, 1955, p. 187.

54. *News from Nowhere,* XVI, 169-170.

Chapter V: Samuel Butler

1. *Method and Results* (New York, 1896), pp. 199-200.

2. *Ibid.,* p. 244.

3. *Ibid.,* p. 240.

4. *Ibid.,* p. 244.

5. Henry Festing Jones, *Samuel Butler, Author of Erewhon: A Memoir* (London, 1919), I, 385.

6. *Ibid.,* II, 41.

7. *Works of Samuel Butler,* Shrewsbury Edition, ed. Henry Festing Jones and A. T. Bartholomew (London, 1923-1926), VI, 17-18. All citations to Butler will refer to this edition.

8. This suggestion is developed in Gertrude Himmelfarb, *Darwin and the Darwinian Revolution* (Garden City, 1962), pp. 159-165.

9. See Basil Willey, *Darwin and Butler: Two Versions of Evolution* (New York, 1960), and U. C. Knoepflmacher, *Religious Humanism and the Victorian Novel* (Princeton, 1965).

10. *Evolution, Old and New,* V, 48.
11. *Luck or Cunning?,* VIII, 8-9.
12. *Evolution, Old and New,* V, 48.
13. I, 237.
14. I, 211.
15. I, 212.
16. I, 212.
17. I, 212.
18. I, 209.
19. I, 210.
20. *Unconscious Memory,* VI, 17.
21. I, 215.
22. I, 215.
23. I, 217.
24. I, 218.
25. I, 217.
26. I, 236-237.
27. I, 237.
28. Preface to Second Edition of *Erewhon,* II, xx.
29. *Life and Habit,* IV, 186-187.
30. II, 178-179.
31. II, 194.
32. II, 197.
33. II, 179.
34. II, 177-178.
35. II, 183.
36. II, 202.
37. II, 203.
38. II, 206.
39. II, 206.
40. II, 214.
41. II, 51.
42. XVI, 139.

Chapter VI: H. G. Wells

1. See the fictional account of life at South Kensington in "A Slip under the Microscope," *The Short Stories of H. G. Wells* (London, 1927), pp. 591-612. This edition will hereafter be referred to as *Short Stories.*
2. Anthony West, "H. G. Wells," *Encounter,* 8:58 (February 1957).

3. See the discussion above of Carlyle's notion of the hero as inventor, pp. 27-28, and of Dickens' story, "Poor Man's Tale of a Patient," above, pp. 52-53.

4. Lydgate in *Middlemarch* is certainly a "round" character, but Lydgate *qua* scientist is not central to the work.

5. New York, 1899, p. 203.

6. *Experiment in Autobiography* (London, 1934), I, 201.

7. *A Modern Utopia* (London, 1905), p. 102.

8. *Experiment in Autobiography*, I, 201.

9. New York, 1902, p. 6.

10. *Anticipations*, p. 97.

11. *A Modern Utopia*, p. 32.

12. Pages 100-101.

13. Page 48.

14. Page 110.

15. Page 111.

16. *Short Stories*, p. 854.

17. *A Modern Utopia*, p. 221.

18. *Short Stories*, p. 322.

19. Pages 324-325.

20. Page 332.

21. Page 324.

22. Page 329.

23. *The Time Machine*, in *Short Stories*, p. 27.

24. *Certain Personal Matters* (London, 1901), pp. 109-110. The essay was reprinted as "Of a Book Unwritten."

25. *Ibid.*, p. 110.

26. *Seven Famous Novels by H. G. Wells* (New York, 1934), pp. 350-352.

27. Page 352.

28. Page 293.

29. Page 351.

30. Pages 296-297.

31. Geoffrey H. Wells, *H. G. Wells: A Bibliography, Dictionary and Subject-Index* (London, 1926), p. 13.

32. Page 274.

33. Page 86.

34. Page 45.

35. Page 236.

36. Page 88.

37. *The Time Machine*, in *Short Stories*, p. 64.

38. *When the Sleeper Wakes*, p. 252.

39. *Short Stories*, p. 844.

40. Pages 852-853.

41. Page 837.
42. Page 800.
43. Wells, *H. G. Wells: A Bibliography*, p. 13.
44. *Seven Famous Novels*, p. 452.
45. Page 400.
46. Pages 514-515.
47. Page 513.
48. *Experiment in Autobiography*, I, 259-260.
49. *The Food of the Gods*, in *Seven Famous Novels*, p. 683.
50. Page 644.
51. Page 682.
52. West, "H. G. Wells," p. 58.
53. *Mind at the End of Its Tether* (London, 1945), p. 4.

Chapter VII: Rudyard Kipling

1. Preface to the Second Edition of *Lyrical Ballads: The Poetical Works of Wordsworth* (London, 1950), p. 738.
2. "Among the Railway Folk" (1888), *From Sea to Sea*, Sussex Ed. (London, 1937-1939), XXII, 268. All citations from Kipling's prose refer to this edition.
3. XXII, 269.
4. *From Sea to Sea*, chaps. xxvi, xxviii, xxxiii.
5. *The Day's Work*, VI, 3.
6. VI, 5.
7. VI, 31.
8. VI, 33.
9. VI, 34.
10. VI, 32.
11. VI, 42.
12. *Traffics and Discoveries*, VII, 243.
13. VII, 225.
14. VII, 243.
15. "The Kipling That Nobody Read," *The Wound and the Bow* (New York, 1941), pp. 105-181.
16. *The Day's Work*, VI, 105.
17. VI, 87.
18. *Rudyard Kipling's Verse: Definitive Edition* (New York, 1940), p. 734. This edition will hereafter be cited as *Verse*.
19. C. E. Carrington, *The Life of Rudyard Kipling* (New York, 1955), p. 197.

20. Curiously, even children's books which take the machine as hero seem inevitably to teach the virtue of self-subordination. See David Riesman's analysis of *Tootle the Engine* in *The Lonely Crowd* (New Haven, 1950), pp. 108-110.

21. "McAndrew's Hymn," *Verse,* p. 125.

22. *Ibid.,* p. 123.

23. "The Wage-Slaves" (1902), *Verse,* p. 307.

24. "A Song of the English" (1893), *Verse,* p. 169.

25. *Verse,* p. 651. Other examples of this genre include "The Trade" (pp. 650-651) and "The Egg-Shell" (pp. 649-650).

26. *A Diversity of Creatures,* IX, 18.

27. IX, 13-14.

28. IX, 3.

29. IX, 34.

30. Ed. J. Shawcross (Oxford, 1907), II, 6.

31. "McAndrew's Hymn," *Verse,* pp. 124-125.

32. *Poems* (London, 1921), p. 265.

33. "Railway Stations," *Fleet Street and Other Poems* (New York, 1909), p. 27.

34. *Verse,* p. 173.

35. "McAndrew's Hymn," *Verse,* p. 124.

36. "The King," *Verse,* p. 374.

37. VIII, 107-108.

38. *Verse,* p. 135.

39. "The Bridge-Builders," VI, 4.

40. Carrington, *Life of Rudyard Kipling,* p. 258.

41. *The Day's Work,* VI, 3.

42. *Verse,* p. 125.

43. *Ibid.*

44. VIII, 115.

45. *Kim,* XXI, 382-383.

46. XXI, 383.

47. *Verse,* p. 121.

48. *Ibid.,* p. 120.

49. J. M. S. Tompkins, *The Art of Rudyard Kipling* (London, 1959), p. 236.

50. *Verse,* pp. 826-827.

51. *Limits and Renewals,* XI, 244-245.

52. XI, 272-273.

53. *Debits and Credits,* X, 313-314.

54. *Verse,* p. 818.

55. XI, 41.

56. XI, 41.

57. XI, 44.

58. "Hymn of Breaking Strain" (1935), *Verse,* pp. 382-383.

Index